My life will never be the same after experiencing the presence of God throughout the pages of this story. It's the only book I've ever read that I had to set down every couple of chapters just to cry and pray. As you read, the God who knows you best will lead you beside still waters and make you lie down in green pastures, bringing personal restoration and refreshment. At times you will laugh; other times you may weep. This book is not theory or a methodology for experiencing God. Max's words come from a heart that intimately knows God and lives in the divine flow of His presence.

—GERMAINE COPELAND
BEST-SELLING AUTHOR, PRAYERS THAT AVAIL MUCH
BOOK SERIES
PRESIDENT, WORD MINISTRIES

What a powerful display of the modern supernatural working of God! Throughout my life I've seen God do some amazing things all over the world, and this story is right up there at the top of the list.

—DR. DAVID SHIBLEY
FOUNDER, GLOBAL ADVANCE

A mind bender! There is no other word for this story but *supernatural*. Read this book, and your prayers will never be the same, for *you* will never be the same.

—CARTER FEATHERSTON
FOUNDER, PURE HEART WEEKENDS
AUTHOR, GOD KNOWS YOUR STORY (AND HE'S NOT MAD!)

What an amazing testimony! It confirms for me the awe and wonder of a holy God who would humble Himself and dwell among us.

—THE LATE MICHAEL CARTER
MORNINGSTAR MINISTRIES

Undeniable proof that God is real and fully present when we cry out to Him.

—BRUCE VAN NATTA
BEST-SELLING AUTHOR, *SAVED BY ANGELS*

Really incredible. It's unexplainable outside of being a God thing. Totally captivating!

—DR. LARRY KOENIG
AUTHOR, *SMART DISCIPLINE: FAST, LASTING
SOLUTIONS FOR YOUR CHILD'S SELF-ESTEEM AND
YOUR PEACE OF MIND*

My life will never be the same! After reading this book, I ended up praying and enjoying the Lord's presence until daylight. I don't know the right words, but I feel so close to the Lord after reading this book and being pulled into God's presence.

—BUZ TREME
HEBREW TEACHER
FOUNDER, WILD OLIVE BRANCHES

A few words that came to mind while reading: supernatural, powerful, inspiring, hopeful, unique. A story that needs telling.

—DENNIS DISNEY
SENIOR VICE PRESIDENT AND CHIEF OPERATING
OFFICER, MAXIMUM ARTIST GROUP

While reading I had to stop occasionally just to cry and pray. This is reinforcing in me that God hears me and knows exactly where I am. He knows all I'm going through and has my answers.

—ROBIN BOQUET
HOUMA, LOUISIANA

I sat down and began to read and didn't get up till I finished the book. It has affected me deeply in ways that I can't really talk about. It opened a place inside me that the message of the story poured into like healing oil.

—Clay McLean
McLean Ministries

Max is a purebred skeptic. As a journalist researching miracle stories, he meticulously questions every last detail to unearth the whole truth and nothing but the truth. But Max's tenacity for facts secures his faith. After I first told him about Josiah, he questioned and double-questioned everything. But when he personally experienced a supernatural encounter involving the young boy, it rocked his world forever. You will experience it too. When Jesus shows up in jaw-dropping ways through a nonverbal autistic boy, one's life can't possibly remain the same.

—Cheryl Ricker
Coauthor, *Rush of Heaven* and *Josiah's Fire*

MAX DAVIS

Jesus, Josiah, & Me

CHARISMA
HOUSE

Visit the author's website at www.maxdavisbooks.com/.

Library of Congress Cataloging-in-Publication Data:
An application to register this book for cataloging has been submitted to the Library of Congress.
International Standard Book Number: 978-1-62999-889-3
E-book ISBN: 978-1-62999-890-9

While the author has made every effort to provide accurate internet addresses at the time of publication, neither the publisher nor the author assumes any responsibility for errors or for changes that occur after publication. Further, the publisher does not have any control over and does not assume any responsibility for author or third-party websites or their content.

Author's note: While Josiah's words have not been changed, punctuation and capitalization have sometimes been added in the interest of clarity.

21 22 23 24 25 — 9 8 7 6 5 4 3 2 1
Printed in the United States of America

And it shall come to pass in the last days, God declares, that I will pour out of My Spirit upon all mankind, and your sons and your daughters shall prophesy [telling forth the divine counsels] and your young men shall see visions (divinely granted appearances), and your old men shall dream [divinely suggested] dreams.

—Acts 2:17, AMPC

CONTENTS

FOREWORD

I FIRST MET MAX in 2011 when he interviewed me for his book *The Insanity of Unbelief: A Journalist's Journey From Belief to Skepticism to Deep Faith.* I can attest firsthand that Max was interested in getting the pure facts of my story to the point he wanted my medical records so he could have a doctor review them. If there was a crack in my story, he was going to find it. Thankfully there were none, and Max published my story.

We have since developed a close friendship and talk often. I've even stayed at his home many times and have met his whole family, including his wife, Alanna. They are both loving and kind as well as dedicated to serving God and fulfilling the assignment He has given them. I've shed tears with Max in his office as we've prayed together. We have shared many moments of awe and wonder over the amazing things we have seen God do.

Max and Alanna are the real deal, and I am so blessed to call them friends. *Jesus, Josiah, and Me* is an amazing supernatural story! It gives undeniable proof that God is real and fully present when we cry out to Him.

—BRUCE VAN NATTA
BEST-SELLING AUTHOR, *SAVED BY ANGELS* AND *A MIRACULOUS LIFE*

Preface

AN AUDACIOUSLY BOLD CLAIM

*God speaks to His people. When He speaks, what
does He reveal? Throughout the Scriptures when God
spoke, it was to reveal something about Himself, His
purposes, or His ways. God's revelations are designed
to bring you into a love relationship with Him.*[1]

—HENRY AND RICHARD BLACKABY AND
CLAUDE KING, *EXPERIENCING GOD*

L ET'S BE HONEST, many of us don't feel God's presence and are
frustrated because our prayers seem to bounce off the walls.
We read our Bibles and try to pray but get bored, distracted, and
just plain weary. It's no secret that life can be brutal at times, and
the unfortunate reality is we tend to equate pain and struggle
with God's absence. Yet as you will see, nothing could be further
from the truth.

I can say with relative confidence, the story you are about
to read is one of the most extraordinary accounts you'll come
across. It falls into the category of "God still speaks directly to
people and still does authentic miracles." It's an out-of-the-box,
supernatural encounter involving me and a nonverbal autistic
boy named Josiah Cullen. My life has been forever altered
because of our interactions, which started in early 2015 when he
was only nine years old.

I have a degree in journalism from the University of
Mississippi and do not accept every story I hear as fact. I hate

embellishment and misinformation. I don't rely on coincidence. If God still does miracles today, as I believe He does, He certainly doesn't need me or anyone else making stuff up. That would only undermine what He can do. Instead, I like to weigh the circumstances involved, consider the credibility of the witnesses, try to verify the details, then determine whether it qualifies as a truly supernatural event.

As my interactions with Josiah increased, they built from powerful and seemingly supernatural to undeniable and mind-blowing. These encounters gave me compelling proof that God is real and longs to spend time with each of us and that He knows us personally—right down to the number of hairs on our heads, what we had for lunch two weeks ago, and how much gas is in our tanks. These encounters also demonstrated how Jesus is fully present in our lives even when things are incredibly painful and circumstances scream He is anything but real and present. We can experience Him in deeper ways than we ever thought possible, and our prayers *can* affect outcomes.

This miraculous account between Josiah and me not only gives evidence of God's reality but reveals the wonder of His presence in our lives. When we experience this reality, even in the most difficult situations everything changes.

Lasting transformation happens. Peace and rest come.

Strongholds are broken. Freedom springs forth, and assignments are given.

Our *maybes* become *yeses*, and life becomes an adventure with God.

Most of all, it is in His presence that we come to know Him intimately.

Now, I'm quite aware everything I just said is an audacious claim. *Undeniable*, *proof*, and *miraculous* are strong words. How can anyone prove God exists, right?

That's a fair question. All I ask is that you read through to the end to get the full impact and then make up your mind. I'm simply recounting my own experience. What you do with it is up to you.

Also, when I say an out-of-the-box supernatural encounter, I do not mean unbiblical or new age in any way. The Holy Scripture is the foundation and final authority in discerning whether any supernatural experience is from God or the deceiver. And there is a very real deceiver. While I am convinced God still speaks today in a variety of ways, the infallible, inspired Word of God is the plumb line for all truth. We should test all things according to 1 John 4:1: "Beloved, do not believe every spirit, but test the spirits, whether they are of God; because many false prophets have gone out into the world." Experiences and prophetic words that have been tested are meant to encourage, illuminate, and warn us and draw us closer to God.

My encounter with Josiah made me worship Jesus more, seek His face more, and search the Scriptures more diligently. It made me cry out for holiness in my life. God used Josiah as a tool to draw me into His presence in a more profound way and to reinforce what God has called me to do in my life. My earnest prayer is that this story will do the same for you.

I have written or cowritten over thirty books. Certainly each book has been a struggle to complete, even a war at times, but nothing compares to what I went through with *Jesus, Josiah, and Me*. It felt as if a full-on attack had been unleashed to prevent this from ending up in your hands. Several times I came to the point of utter despair and giving up. It was crazy.

As you read for yourself, you'll understand why opposing forces wanted to keep this story from being told. Read on and enjoy the story.

Brace yourself, though. You may never be the same!

1

SOMETHING COMPELLING

*The Universal Presence is a fact. God is here. The whole
universe is alive with His life....And always He is trying to get
our attention, to reveal Himself to us, to communicate with us.*
—A. W. TOZER, *THE PURSUIT OF GOD*

January 8, 2015

A SINGLE PHONE CALL started this incredible journey and
friendship. At about 9:00 a.m., as I walked around the path
at Perkins Road Community Park in Baton Rouge, Louisiana,
I dialed Cheryl Ricker, a fellow writer who lives in Rochester,
Minnesota. I had just finished reading a book she collaborated
on and wanted to tell her how much it impacted me. We connected as fellow writers, discussing agents and publishers. We
talked about the fact that we were living in the biblical end times
and that we needed to be faithful with our writing gifts.

We also talked about our newest writing projects. While most
of my books had been nonfiction, in those early weeks of January,
I was racing to meet a major publisher's deadline for my novel
Dead Dog Like Me. Go check it out. The copyright is 2015. The
year before, I had coauthored *The Impressionist*, another novel.

As we continued talking, Cheryl told me she was in the beginning stages of writing a book with Tahni Cullen, the mother of
a nine-year-old autistic boy named Josiah who communicated
by tapping words with one finger onto a laminated cardboard
keyboard or a tablet. Josiah's words, some believed, had spiritual impact. Cheryl gave me the quick elevator pitch, going into
very little detail. Nothing was asked of me, other than prayer
and advice. Our conversation lasted about an hour and ended

at approximately 10:00 a.m. I had lots to do and hurried into my day. With my deadline looming, I forgot all about our call.

For years, the office where I did my writing was a twelve-by-twelve-foot metal shed next to the house on our forty acres of family property. The little shed was my place of retreat, but now it and our house of roughly two decades had been torn down so my wife, Alanna, and I could build an Acadian cottage. This would be our dream home and truly a writer's paradise.

In the meantime, however, we were staying in a mobile home in the woods about a football field away from the construction site. I had created a makeshift office inside the mobile home, but it was extremely tiny—more like a closet with a curtain in the open doorway.

Have you ever tried building a new home and living in a crowded temporary one while undertaking a book project? As you can imagine, this made it even more difficult to have the space and quiet I needed to concentrate for extended periods.

Let's just say I was feeling the pressure.

That afternoon, I got an email from Cheryl. She had called Tahni at 11:00 a.m., after talking with me, and relayed to her some of our discussion about being faithful with our writing in these end times. At 3:00 p.m., Tahni's son arrived home from a special school for autistic children. Before she could talk to him or find out how his day went, Josiah shot over to his tablet and started typing. Tahni saw his references to "God" and "note takers" and got the impression her son might be alluding to a particular person. She asked, "Josiah, does this have anything to do with Max?" Though he had never met or even heard of me before, he typed:

> Lots to do with Max, yes.

In the email on my screen, I read the things Josiah had written about me. Cheryl noted that Tahni was concerned about sending me Josiah's typed thoughts since Tahni wasn't even sure they were relevant. My eyes moved down the screen as I tried to imagine a young autistic boy plunking out these words, one letter at a time. I didn't know him or his family. What did he look like? Why would he be sending me anything?

His message read:

> Make no mistake. My arguments for God and Jesus and Holy Spirit are not for church people...but for those in this earth that say God is not here anymore.... It is for saving banished people from hell....My Jesus

wants note takers to name him as a king. He is King. He is daring. He is active. He is artful....My mom is dalet to this careful named savior. My mom is a dalet....His nails are his minutes in Heaven making answers to messes that man has made.

He certainly had my interest. I had to admit, there was something compelling about the way he phrased things. His words had depth and weight. I sat up and kept reading.

My name is no one, but my happiness is in my nothing-ness....Jesus is best known through his nails, his broken heart for mankind. Messiah is making his kingdom become now, not then, through people that need a savior—not mental saving but monumental saving.

While this already had my attention, I was completely unprepared for what came next. It was the response Josiah gave when Tahni asked if this message had anything to do with me.

Lots to do with Max, yes. He is definitely not only a major novel writer; he knows valuable sameness is not always the best approach.

Stop.
Right.
There.
A "major novel writer"? After getting only my first name, the kid already knew I was a writer, and not just any writer but a novel writer. The fact that I make a living as an author is unbelievable all by itself. In high school I was a D student in English. If my classmates had voted on who was least likely to succeed in the literary arts, I would've been a serious contender. And to Josiah, "Max" could have been anybody—a coach, a teacher, an agent, a pastor, a friend, an astronaut. There are nearly seven billion people on this planet, yet he identified my exact profession.

When he wrote, "He knows valuable sameness is not always the best approach," that was even more personal, applying to my career in ways few people understand. I cringe when aspiring authors ask how I became an author, because my path has been so unorthodox. When my first book was released, years before the internet and social media, I did something few others even considered. I sold it directly to thirty-five hundred non-bookstore outlets—gift shops, gas stations, grocery stores, you name it. This was hard work, but as a result, we moved thousands of copies outside of traditional bookstores! I am always considering unusual methods of getting my work into readers' hands, even those who don't usually read. Also, my books have creative titles to go along with my unique writing style. In *Dead Dog Like Me*, for example, I broke so many literary rules it wasn't funny, but I did it on purpose. As Josiah mentioned, my approach is not the same as anyone else's.

Wide-eyed, I read over the email again. To say I was intrigued would be an understatement. Think of it this way: What if I didn't write novels? What if I wasn't even a writer? What if I did things by the book? You see? It would've been so easy for Josiah to get one detail wrong, and then I could have blown off the whole thing.

But he didn't.

And I couldn't.

As I struggled with a deadline and my own insecurities, this seemed like just the sort of encouragement God would send me. How else would I, in Louisiana, be getting a message from a complete stranger, a boy who couldn't even talk, over twelve hundred miles away in wintry Minnesota?

Still, my skeptical, journalistic nature kicked in, and I figured surely someone had tipped the boy off. Maybe Cheryl had given the Cullens information about me. Or they had gone to my website and checked me out. That had to be it.

Unable to let it rest, I contacted Tahni right away and started questioning her. I wanted to know more about her and her son. I wanted to get to the bottom of this.

2

TAHNI'S STORY

*Spiritual growth, in a sense, is simply increasing
our capacity to experience the presence of God.*
—JOHN ORTBERG, GOD IS CLOSER THAN YOU THINK

October 4, 2005

THE DAY OUR blue-eyed baby boy was born, we knew what we
would call him. My husband and I had labored over names.
Then one day in a work meeting, I heard someone say the name
Josiah. With his daddy's name being Joseph, I thought it would
be a great complement, and Joe agreed. The meaning in Hebrew
was "fire of the Lord." That settled it. Josiah it would be.

Through the next two years, our happy, social, curly-headed
blond boy met his medical milestones. He called us "Mama" and
"Dada" and used words such as "banana."

Just a little before his second birthday, it all changed.

——————

August 18, 2007

Josiah stopped looking us in the eyes. He suddenly lost his words
and other skills. He didn't respond to his name when called. He
no longer played with his toys properly and just spun wheels and
turned light switches on and off. It was as if his pilot light went
out.

And this was our "fire of the Lord."

A handful of months later, a pediatric psychologist diagnosed him with autism spectrum disorder—no known cause, no known cure.

We cried out to the Lord. Despite our laid-low praying and every kind of intervention and therapy we could throw at this "unresolvable" problem, Josiah was labeled "low-functioning, nonverbal, and severe." Joe and I were devastated. Even while we clung to the Lord for hope, Josiah had complete meltdowns, oftentimes in public places such as the mall. While people shot me judgmental stares, I spoke gentle words over my son, not even sure if he could understand, and took him to safe spaces away from sensory stimulation.

At age five, Josiah was still nonverbal, and Joe and I wondered if he would be one of those on the autism spectrum who never learned to speak. I tried teaching him to spell by pointing out letters and pronouncing words but didn't see much progress. As a minister in our church, I read the Bible and parables to him and spoke to him of spiritual concepts. I had no idea if any of it was registering. Yet even on the days I felt like giving up, I chose to presume intelligence. Just because my son couldn't speak didn't mean he couldn't think.

September 15, 2012

Our breakthrough came only weeks before Josiah's seventh birthday. After working with him by pointing at letters for about a year, I watched my "low-functioning" son type a sentence on his tablet independently for the first time:

> God is a good gift giver.

Stunned, I gasped for breath. This was a total miracle, so far beyond anything we had seen to that point. It was still a tedious process, Josiah circling his finger and landing it one letter at a time on the keyboard, but he was expressing himself on a level we never imagined. In that moment, God's supernatural power intercepted and interrupted our lives in an unexplainable, yet undeniable, way.

And it was only the beginning.

———

January 8, 2015

By the time Max Davis called, seeking answers about me and my son, God had already taken me on an adventure that included my laying aside my own reputation, surrendering what people thought of me, and learning to be discerning. Even when I tried to be obedient to the Holy Spirit, it took some courage to share Josiah's writings—with people I already knew, yes, and especially with a complete stranger in Louisiana.

Josiah was experiencing things I had no framework for. Even though I had worked in ministry for many years and thought I had a handle on the proper "God formulas," it was still terrifying at times, yet all arrows pointed to God. For this reason, I agreed to partner with Cheryl Ricker on our book, *Josiah's Fire: Autism Stole His Words, God Gave Him a Voice.*

That afternoon in early January, I simply passed on Josiah's message to Cheryl.

And she forwarded it to Max Davis.

Of course, it wasn't simple, since I had to jump through my own emotional hoops to even share what came spontaneously from my son. What if it didn't mean anything to Max? What if he didn't even write novels? Then Max contacted me, and his skepticism was obvious from the start. He asked questions over and over, grilling me to see if I was tricking him or something. Honestly I wasn't even sure I liked him at first. He hurt my feelings a little. I didn't need this! I was just trying to be obedient to God.

No, I made clear, I wasn't after money, his or anyone else's.

Did I find purpose in this? Sure, I found meaning in helping my son express himself and in following God's directions. If I could, though, I'd do it all anonymously and be just as content.

Fame? I definitely didn't need it, not when I spent most of my waking hours simply caring for Josiah—feeding him, changing his diapers, and trying to make it through the day. It was already hard enough for Joe and me to find any quality alone time without drawing more attention to the Cullen home.

To address any doubts Max still had, I sent him this email:

> Max, I can assure you that I have never told Josiah that you are a writer. I would not lie to you or try to deceive you. He is still a nine-year-old boy with autism. Most things like this that he brings up, I don't even dream about discussing with him. Again, understand that I don't "check people out" spiritually like that through Josiah. I'm extremely careful not to manipulate or lead like that. I may ask him things about God, Jesus, Heaven or questions about spiritual things, but things for other people, if he has anything, just unfold on their own. *You have to think back about how this started.* Cheryl calls me to tell me about you contacting her out of the blue and just wondering if we could be in prayer about her agent and the direction to go with the book's audience. Josiah comes home from school. *I have not even talked with him*, and like he often does, he just starts writing after I asked him how his day went. He starts writing about a general topic and alludes to a person. From there, I ask, does this have anything to do with Max? That's it. I would stand before God Himself and tell you exactly the same thing. I really have nothing to gain ever from trying to force anything. Cheryl knows my heart through this long process, we just keep surrendering to God, and

we believe He will guide us. I have no motives to fabricate anything, assuredly. :)

Max wasn't the only one grappling with the realities of God seeing and knowing him so personally. So was I. It was an ongoing process, discovering a Father so grand and yet so detailed that He has written our names on the palms of His hands. He knows. He sees. He is aware of the precise gifts we need, and sometimes He moves heaven and earth to deliver them to us!

Yes, as Josiah said, "God is a good gift giver."

3

THE TIP OF THE ICEBERG

*In God's Presence, we've come before the One who
speaks worlds into being, who delights in speaking
new worlds of being into our very souls.*
—LEANNE PAYNE, *THE HEALING PRESENCE*

January 8, 2015

AT THE RISK of offending Tahni, I had looked for any loop-
hole in her story, and she responded patiently. Despite the
skeptic in me, she conveyed no ulterior motives or reasons for
manipulating her son's messages. She never asked for recog-
nition or compensation. She didn't ask one thing of me, other
than to respect her family and what it was enduring. She showed
strong, healthy boundaries of protection over her son, and as a
parent myself, I respected that. I had an adult deaf son, diagnosed at thirteen months old, and I knew the years of anguish
we went through together. I heard in Tahni's voice that same
weary bravery.

The process had not been easy on the Cullen family—that was
obvious—and I was sure Tahni and Joe would happily take peace
and rest and the healing of their son over any of this. Yet because
Tahni was obedient when the Holy Spirit moved through Josiah,
she too had become a willing vessel.

Adding to all that, the unusual wording Josiah used had not
seemed like something a person could or would make up. His
afternoon message to me gave a bit of insight into his thoughts
about God. He was on target biblically and was all about glori-
fying Jesus and saving the lost from hell.

That evening in our mobile home, my thoughts spun. Despite

my fears and insecurities, I knew God was speaking to me. Concerns about my deadline were washed away by the realization that He was with me. I was not left to do this all on my own.

That was a good thing—a very good thing.

Not so long before, He had told me to begin writing novels in addition to my nonfiction. I could still recall that night with clarity, though at the time, it made no sense in the natural realm. It was hard enough for this former D student to excel at journalism. How much harder would storytelling be? Writing fiction involved skills such as plotting, pacing, characterization, and dialogue.

There was no more second-guessing. Through Josiah, God had confirmed that holy calling.

As I read Josiah's message again, the words amazed me. It was significant when he said, "My Jesus wants note takers to name him as a king." Writing had never been merely a dream of mine. It was an assignment. I didn't write books just to weave captivating, creative yarns, though that was certainly an important element. No, God called me specifically to write what He told me to write. So I studied, prayed, listened to the Holy Spirit, and took notes. That was what Jesus wanted, as Josiah said. I believed it was what He wanted from all of us. We could all become His notetakers. We could all hear His voice and receive His assignments for our lives.

This was powerful stuff, fueled by supernatural purpose—and expressed through an autistic boy!

Tahni had detailed for me how her son's process worked, and I imagined Josiah's darting blue eyes as he held his tablet. Thanks to rapid prompting method, or RPM, initially he had learned to communicate by stabbing his fingers at plastic stencil letters. He now typed with one finger, one letter at a time, onto either an electronic tablet or a laminated keyboard. This took

incredible effort, as his arms and body flailed around. It was difficult for him to sit still for long periods, and his mother often had to steady his arm and remind him to stay focused while he typed. It was a long and arduous process. Tahni also explained that Josiah had no independent access to the internet. His jerking motions were so profound it would be nearly impossible for him to access the internet even if he wanted to.

When Josiah had a heavenly vision, an angelic visitation, or a prophetic message, he spelled it out on his tablet, often in the middle of the night. After he made noises to rouse Tahni from her sleep, she went to his bedside to help him type what he'd experienced. God spoke through him to others with highly personal details, details that were impossible for him to know unless revealed by the Holy Spirit. It was also common for Josiah to have a message or vision in the daytime, right in the middle of something else. When this happened, he often led his mother to the couch or table. She sat beside him, letting his elbow rest on her leg as she held up the tablet and steadied his arm. He then painstakingly pecked out his sentences.

One other thing jumped out from Josiah's message to me. Twice he had described his mother in an odd way:

> My mom is dalet to this careful named savior. My
> mom is a dalet.

After earning my bachelor's in journalism from Ole Miss, I
went on to study at Oral Roberts University and earned a mas-
ter's in theology from American Bible College and Seminary.
I knew from my training that *dalet* is the fourth letter of the
Hebrew alphabet and means door. Indeed, Tahni was the
doorway for Josiah, selflessly facilitating the process to get his
messages to whom they were intended for. I found Josiah's use
of *dalet* astoundingly accurate in context. I figured his parents probably listened to Bible teaching in their home, allowing
Josiah to pick up a Hebrew word here or there. Tahni insisted
that was not the case, that they never talked about or studied
Hebrew in their home or around Josiah. He had no theological
training, and *dalet* was incredibly specific. It is divinely fitting he
would use that word to describe his mother.

I would soon encounter more Hebrew and more surprises
from him.

Josiah's first message to me, though brief, was quite amazing—
and it was only the tip of the iceberg. If that had been my only
encounter with Josiah, I would have been deeply grateful.

Yet there was still more ahead—oh, so much more!

Over the next three and a half years, I received and printed
out approximately twenty pages, typed, single-spaced, with
words from Josiah. They led me on the most remarkable journey
of my life, shattering any doubts that God was real and fully
involved in our lives. They strengthened my faith and reaffirmed
in a fresh way that my life here on earth is ultimately about my
eternal life in heaven, that the Holy Spirit still guides and speaks
today. More than anything, Josiah's words always led me back to
Jesus and the Bible, seeking more of God. His Hebrew words and

deep biblical insights unveiled pathways to experiencing God's presence and to the power of prayer.

Incredibly, I found out while writing this book, Josiah couldn't even read the Bible for himself. When asked how he learned the things he shared, he gave a simple reply:

Jesus and angels taught me.

I wasn't sure why God allowed His words to come to me through His amazing child, but I was humbled and grateful, knowing it was my assignment to get His message out so others could be encouraged as well. Josiah spoke in his own autistic way. His words were unusually beautiful and creative and took a little time to ponder before grasping. Often his prophetic messages were wrapped in the middle of another message or paragraph. I had to read them slowly to absorb their full power, and I ask you to do the same as you encounter them in these pages.

My next message from Josiah came only eight days later.

4

SACRED MOTEL TIMES

I cannot for the life of me twist the text to prove that the power of God in the supernatural gifts of the Holy Spirit was limited to the times of the early church. However, it is not just for me a matter of exegesis, but of personal experience.
—R. T. Kendall, *Holy Fire*

January 12, 2015

DAYS BEFORE THAT second message arrived, I was still facing my deadline—"a major novel," as Josiah put it, with a major publisher. I knew godly supernatural encounters often helped people deal with physical realities, and Josiah's first message greatly encouraged me. I was on the right path. Finishing this novel was important, and God was with me to overcome my own sense of inadequacy.

During the past nine months, as our home was being built, due to limited space and privacy and my inability to concentrate, I often drove over to the coast of Mississippi to write. I probably made that trip an average of two times per month, using the solitude to hyper-focus and block out distractions.

Days before receiving Josiah's second message, I headed down once more.

I liked the Mississippi Gulf Coast because it was quiet and uncrowded and I could walk for miles and miles along the well-lit promenade paralleling the ocean. Plus, I had a little LED flashlight that clipped onto my hat for strolling the beach at night. Walking was a critical part of my writing, since, to use Josiah's words, "sameness is not always the best approach." I spent hours with a clipboard in hand, jotting down my thoughts as I went.

Later I transcribed my notes onto the computer. It was a great system for my ADD mind.

That January on the Gulf, I checked into a quaint motel located just off the beach under a cluster of shade trees. It wasn't at all like the hotels I visited while at conferences, meetings, and interviews. There was something raw and real and inspirational about this place, a certain ambiance that sparked my creativity. The motel's owners knew me well and even read my books. All I had to do was call and say I was on the way, and they got my room ready. It was usually the same room number: 120. It was very quiet and clean, with a bed, desk, sofa, and minifridge. Since 2010 I had gone to this motel on a regular basis.

Once I arrived, I followed my regular routine. I never wavered from it. This routine involved five steps upon entering the room. First, I took out my cell phone or laptop, went online to YouTube, and linked to peaceful, worship music. Each YouTube clip was anywhere from five minutes to two hours. I then let the music play continuously, creating an atmosphere for prayer and praise. Some people called it soaking worship. Not once did I play the radio, insert a CD, or use an MP3 player. I was way too old-school for that. I made my playlist; that's what I did on every visit. I didn't do this just five out of ten times or eight out of ten times but every single time I went to the motel.

Music is a powerful tool in God's kingdom. In the Old Testament, when the king of Israel, the king of Edom, and Jehoshaphat asked for a word from the Lord, the prophet Elisha told them no at first. Later he changed his mind and instructed them to bring him a musician. "And when the musician played, the hand of the LORD came upon him. And he [Elisha] said, 'Thus says the LORD...'"[1] and gave them the word. On another occasion, as Jehoshaphat went into battle, he "appointed men to sing to the LORD and to praise him for the splendor of his holiness....As they began to sing and praise, the LORD set ambushes against the men of Ammon and Moab and Mount Seir who were invading Judah, and they were defeated."[2]

In the New Testament, when Paul and Silas were chained up in that dark, damp, dirty dungeon, they sang praises to God, and He caused an earthquake that loosed their chains.[3] Playing praise-and-worship music and singing a cappella were more than just ways of filling the room with pretty, moving songs. They ushered in the presence of God. That's why this was such an important part of my routine, my system.

Second, I always took along my Bible and a sackful of Christian books. Among the books the Lord was currently using to speak to me, there were invariably four or five miracle-testimony books I'd already systematically critiqued and concluded were authentic accounts of God. I had collected these miracle stories since the early 1980s and had a whole section on my office bookshelf dedicated to them. If you were around me for any length of time, you were going to hear about them. My life was about miracle stories. They were so ingrained in me that they became part of who I was. As the worship music played throughout my motel room, I studied the Bible, read my miracle testimonies and other faith-building books, and created an atmosphere conducive to hearing from God.

Third, after creating an atmosphere of faith, I poured out my heart to God, worshipping Him and pacing while praying in the Spirit. Sometimes I fell on my knees or lay flat on my face. It got intense. It was not a recreational time. It was spiritual warfare. During these prayer times, I sought the Lord's direction on how to move forward with my writing and with my life. "I can't do this, God. Only You can!" I cried out. "Show me what to write. Write through me. Show me how to live. Speak to me through Your Word and Spirit."

Fourth, after prayer, with pen and clipboard in hand, I went for long walks on the beach, often late into the night, writing as the Spirit of God illuminated my mind. I usually walked in two- or three-hour increments but sometimes up to six-hour increments. I had walked eight hours in one stretch. Of course, I stopped to rest along the way.

I looked forward to my motel times with great anticipation. I simply couldn't wait. I knew I would rather spend time alone with God than do anything else. At the old house, the shed office, or the trailer, it was difficult to listen to worship music for extended, uninterrupted periods, even with earphones. My purpose in going to the coast was not to vacation but specifically to pour out my soul, recharge spiritually, and write. I had to hear from the Lord. When I was desperate for long, concentrated time with God, one of my favorite places to go was that quaint little motel.

Again, these steps were my system. I followed them every time.

OK, did you get all that?

The moment I returned home to Louisiana, a second email came to me, full of more words from young Josiah.

———

January 16, 2015

That Friday, as I opened the email and started reading, my heart thumped in my chest. Josiah's second communication was nearly two pages long, timely in ways I couldn't possibly ignore. Apart from my wife, Alanna, no one else knew where I had been the past few days or what I'd been doing. That would have defeated the whole purpose of my going away. But God knew. Yes, that quickly became clear.

There on my laptop screen, the message began:

> Max is a night man to make his writing a lot at night. And he likes banding his music for sacred times at motels.

Gulp.

I chewed on that for a moment.

The boy's description of me as a "night man...writing a lot at night" was 100 percent accurate, my exact routine on the coast. Then he added that I was someone who "likes banding his music for sacred times." In other words, my playlists helped prepare a sacred atmosphere, which was my goal when I put them together. And Josiah didn't say I just listened to or played my music. He said I liked "banding" my music. It was an odd word choice, but I knew *banding* was a biblical term that means linked, connected, or grouped together. *Band*, *banded*, or *banding* appeared over forty times in the Bible. For example, in Acts 23:12 (KJV), the apostle Paul said the Jews "banded" together against him to try and kill him. When Josiah wrote that I was banding my music, he meant I was linking or connecting my playlist. It was exactly what I had done at the motel, and my whole reason was to set a tone "for sacred times" of prayer.

"C'mon," I thought. "How amazing is that?"

Josiah hadn't stated these sacred times were at my house, or an apartment, or a condo, or a hotel. No, he distinctly used the word *motels*. He was absolutely right. Hotels were usually made up of hundreds of rooms, multiple floors, inside staircases, elevators, and interior halls. Motels commonly had one or two floors, with guests accessing rooms directly from the parking lot. I had never once stayed in a coastal hotel for my sacred times. I always stayed in a motel.

I was fully awake. The specifics in just those first two lines were incredible!

As I considered the contents of the email, my investigative tendency was to break down the facts in order to find evidence and to silence claims of exaggeration or lunacy. I realized how critical the message's personal details were because they weren't reliant on any feelings or subjective reasoning. Josiah's pinpoint accuracy could only come through the Holy Spirit.

I had been on the Gulf Coast, and he was in Minnesota. Yet what I had been doing matched what the boy described.

Wait, though. Had Josiah somehow seen a beach picture I posted online? Would that explain it? No, I realized, I'd never posted anything about staying in motels or banding my music or going away for sacred times. Plus, Josiah was unable to personally access or even scroll the internet. He had no way of knowing any of these details of my last few days, particularly what was going on inside the motel.

I called Alanna over and shared the email with her. She was just as blown away. Of course, my skeptical self wanted to know if she had possibly connected with Tahni or Josiah Cullen during the last week. Had she inadvertently passed along information Josiah could've latched onto for this message? But that was ridiculous. Tahni and Josiah didn't even know who my wife was and certainly didn't have her contact information. Plus, Alanna never checks my emails and barely even knew what was going on between Josiah and me. It was still early in this whole adventure. No, my wife assured me, she'd had no contact at all with the Cullens.

In fact, three more years would pass before my first face-to-face encounter with Josiah—and it wouldn't go quite as expected!

We will get to that, I promise. Back to the email...

———

Convinced God was moving through this boy, I kept reading:

> Warring for gutsy margins to move in his best awesome daring way.

I recognized *warring* as a word referring to prayer. In the movie *War Room*, released later that same year, the war room was a designated place in the house for prayers of spiritual warfare. The cries to God that went forth from that room deeply impacted lives and availed much. The Bible made clear that Jesus expected us to pray and spend time alone with Him. He affirmed this when He said, "But when you pray, go into your room, close the door and pray to your Father, who is unseen. Then your Father, who sees what is done in secret, will reward you."[4]

In my prayers at the motel, I too had been "warring for gutsy margins," as Josiah said. I had warred in the Spirit, praying in my "best awesome daring way," as he said, about how I should move in my writing and in my life. Through Josiah's simple, childlike description, I knew deep in my soul that my Father had seen my prayers in secret.

How could that not put a huge smile on my face?

In the very next sentence, Josiah continued:

> Max, vagueness is not your miracle stories. They need your sage simplicity to name them as miracles...you are loud in heaven for miracles...major big mighty loud miracles.

The miracle stories I'd collected for decades were *my* miracle stories. They didn't make my shelf if they were vague. They had to be specific and documented. Reading over them encouraged my faith and led to my own supernatural encounters. In my motel room, I had read through some of these testimonies to prepare me for prayer. David wrote in Psalms, "Once again I'll go over what GOD has done, lay out on the table the ancient wonders; I'll ponder all the things you've accomplished, and give a long, loving look at your acts."[5]

I believe that remembering the works of God in our lives is an intentional faith-building act. Rather than just a one-time thing, it is recounting over and over the stories of what God has done for us. This is essential to preparing our hearts to enter His presence.

When Josiah wrote, "They need your sage simplicity to name them as miracles," he described exactly what I did each time I read these stories, writing them out and breaking them down from a journalistic viewpoint. If I was going to proclaim God's work, I wanted to tell of His "big mighty loud miracles," as Josiah said.

"What are the odds?" I wondered. "Josiah had nailed my complete routine!"

Yes, I went to motels to connect with God and to band my music together for sacred times. I did warfare, praying in the Spirit for direction, and I read and reread my miracle stories to bolster my faith. At night I did my walking and writing. It was my long-established routine. On this trip, while I'd been having one of my more spiritually intense visits to the Gulf Coast, Josiah had been in his house in Minnesota typing out a detailed vision of my sacred motel times. That right there made me want to stop what I was doing and cry out to God!

Soak that in. God saw me.

And He sees *you*.

Let me pause right here to say, regardless of how you feel, your prayers are also heard by God. Believe it. It's true. Jesus said it, and Josiah's messages confirmed it. One of the ways God rewards us is with His presence and direction in our lives. This is a result of not just praying for timid little answers but of "warring for gutsy margins," as Josiah said, praying for God to move not just in mediocre ways but in His "best awesome daring way."

You are *not* alone.

He rewards you as you seek Him.

Your fervent prayers are *not* in vain.

By writing this book about Josiah's words to me, I am using my "simplicity to name them as miracles," in Josiah's words. Just recounting these personal stories for you makes me want to go be alone with God all over again. I hope it makes you want that too. His arms are open wide. Believe me, there's even more to uncover from Josiah's second message, but it will have to wait for the next chapter. I'll meet you there when you're ready.

We're just getting started!

5

BIG HAND, BARNS, AND
POPPING HOUSES

To be much for God, we must be much with God.
—Leonard Ravenhill, *Why Revival Tarries*

January 16, 2015

A s I scanned the rest of Josiah's message, I was stunned. It included things about my wife and me, about our home and current living situation. It was stuff Josiah had no way of knowing.

Lord, how is this even possible? I prayed. You are incredible!

At that point in time, Alanna and I had been married for over twenty years. Our first grandchild, Sam, had just been born, and we were excited about entering this next season of our lives in our new place. Our property sat on the edge of town. We were only ten minutes from stores, restaurants, and schools. We still lived in our temporary mobile home. When we stepped out the door, pretty much the first thing we saw across the lane was our barn.

My father-in-law raised about a half dozen milk goats and a small army of grazing chickens. Eggs were a daily part of my breakfast menu, oftentimes as I sat and watched the news. In addition, we had a couple of peacocks, a wild turkey that showed up every morning on our front porch, and a spoiled poodle named Teddy, who ran around chasing squirrels. On top of the animal sounds around us, we had the regular racket of construction as our new home progressed.

Despite any little inconveniences, the end goal was in sight. It would be a beautiful place for welcoming family, friends, and guests. As a couple, we had learned to work, play, and pray together. We had our conflicts, like most people, but we got through them and grew closer to each other. We were best friends and a spiritual duo.

A few years earlier this was confirmed when a friend had a remarkable dream about us. He was so overwhelmed that he rushed to our house to share the details with us around our kitchen table. The dream came to him as a Japanese anime cartoon. In it my character was a big hand wearing a metal gauntlet. I was a weapon. Alanna was my wielder, the one who guided the weapon. As a professional CPA, an auditor, Alanna knows how to focus things. She's also in tune with the Holy Spirit. Her job was to direct my fist for maximum impact, and we fought as a team. When the two of us were in sync and resonated in battle, spikes burst out of the gauntlet, making it even more effective. This hand/weapon represented my calling and gift of writing. I was a powerful fist hitting my targets, our friend told us, but I needed Alanna's focus and accuracy as I swung all over the place and blasted through things.

Both Alanna and I felt the dream was prophetic, a huge confirmation of the inner workings of our relationship—so much so that we commissioned an artist to do a drawing of the dream. I hung it in my office as an encouraging reminder of the calling on both of our lives and our critical need to stay in sync.

With a renewed sense of purpose and identity, Alanna and I began to resonate as a team on a higher level. I needed her, and she needed me. She couldn't transform into a gauntlet and blast with the same raw power, and I couldn't become the wielder and have her same focused precision. This is what the apostle Paul talked about when he said, "As believers, we are one body, one spirit, but have many members. Should the foot say, 'I'm not of the body because I'm not a hand'?"[1] No. If we were all the same, where would the body be? In the body of Christ, the church, we each had a vital role to play, a mission to accomplish, just as God set it up. None could boast, because we all seriously needed one another.

In the Davis household, I was the hand/weapon. Alanna was my wielder.

Together we collaborated to hit our targets.

These intimate bits of our background, home, and marriage tumbled through my thoughts as I continued reading Josiah's email that day in early January:

> Nice big hand named in heaven as God's biter of language. May I explain? That is, it packs a powerful punch. Max hits targets. You have a real hand trained for war.

It was uncanny. Once again, the boy had nailed it, and neither Alanna nor I could ignore the correlation between the "nice big hand named in heaven" and the drawing of the gauntlet on my wall. My job as a writer was to jot down, process, and edit words, and as a "biter of language," I prayed daily I would be one who "packs a powerful punch" and "hits targets." The dream and the email had arrived years apart, yet their parallel imagery was astounding. Both Alanna and I found it so personal and meaningful.

I straightened in my seat. The odds against this being some sort of coincidence or trick were really beginning to stack up.

Next, Josiah wrote:

> Are you a barn man ever, Max? I see animals but can't say you live on a farm. Do you safely bask ever at a farm? Weeds in my vision on that one.

It was funny to even think of a non-speaking autistic boy asking me these questions. He had no idea what I saw every time I walked out our front door. Our barn and our host of animals were things we loved about our property. Yes, I did "safely bask" here, but he was right when he added, "Can't say you live on a farm." Even with a barn, goats, and chickens, we never said we lived on a farm. We were located on that glorious border between the country and suburbs. No wonder the poor kid had trouble getting a clear image, stating outright, "Weeds in my vision on that one."

Well, we did have some weeds around the place, but I really hoped he wasn't suggesting I get to work on those.

With a grin, I moved on expectantly, but Josiah's next words puzzled me at first:

> Housing upper popping like his home is popping, Mom, lots of popping like naming pop pop pop.

He sounded confused, and so was I—until later, when I walked outside for a look at our construction underway and heard the nail guns popping. They were so loud at times I had to shout to be heard or had to cover my ears just to think. It was very distracting, especially for me as a writer. "Pop pop pop." As our new home was going up, that noise continued loudly for weeks. It was mind-boggling to me that Josiah, trying to communicate what he meant to his mother, painted the picture perfectly. A boy twelve hundred miles away not only saw our barn and our animals but also heard "lots of popping" as work was done on our cottage!

Had Josiah ever been to my house?

No, never. Even at highway level, if you drove by our address, you couldn't see any of the details he described, not with our place set so far back off the road.

"Oh," I imagine doubters scoffing, "he could have just googled it."

No, he couldn't have. Nor could his mother. I did my homework, and here was the real kicker. At the time of Josiah's message, Google Maps for our property was dated several years prior. Our house going up and doing all that popping wasn't even under construction when those satellite images were spliced together. They showed only hazy images of the old house surrounded by trees. Our dream cottage wouldn't appear until 2016, when Google updated its files, a full year after I received Josiah's email. Even then, you couldn't find more than trees and a roof in the satellite views, and certainly not any animals—not one. I tried.

This next part was so obvious it seemed silly to even point it out, but there was also no way anyone could hear nail guns on Google Maps. Yet by the divine power of the almighty God, this boy way up north had heard my house popping way down south.

"I'm telling you," Tahni later said to me, "he just knows stuff."

After that, every time I passed by a house under construction and heard that popping—"pop pop pop"—I was deeply moved, sometimes to tears.

Can you hear it too? Please tell me you're getting all this as you read along.

Do you ever think God has forgotten you? Do you ever worry that He's done working in and through you? Impossible! He is the God who never sleeps. He is always at work, able to reveal Himself in countless, unique ways. "For we are His workmanship, created in Christ Jesus for good works, which God prepared beforehand that we should walk in them."[2]

You serve an all-knowing God, a Creator.

He knows right where you are. He knows the purposes He has for you.

Even when the cares of this life weigh you down, even when your own spiritual senses are dulled by despair, your Father in heaven has His eyes and ears turned your way. He wants to make His love and His plans clear, if only you'll quiet yourself, turn toward Him, and listen.

6

EAT LIKE A BIG GUY

And in the meantime, out of this abiding, Jesus
transforms us. Our identity begins to coalesce, not out of
doing, but out of living with a good friend for a number of
years and simply finding we have become more like him.
—Brent Curtis and John Eldredge, *The Sacred Romance*

January 16, 2015

As I READ the last half of the message, I ran across God's playful sense of humor in strangely specific portions such as this:

> Max basically is begging God for eggs, not worn out yokes....Eggs are his loud made love.

Wow. It was true my father-in-law raised chickens, but not many people knew it. It wasn't something detectable on Google Maps, and I'd never put pictures of chickens or eggs on social media. What was even more significant was that we had a daily supply of eggs. I'm talking about eggs with the most amazingly rich, deep yellow-orange yolks, packed with all the protein and nutrients the chickens got from grazing for worms, insects, grasses, soil, and so on. In addition, they were fertilized by the roosters that grazed with the hens. The eggs were certainly "not worn out yokes," in Josiah's words, due to any processing or sitting on a grocery shelf.

Josiah was expressing that the eggs I got were fresh, and that was a fact. I was a routine person, and just as I banded my music every time I got to the motel, I cooked fresh eggs for Alanna and myself nearly every morning. I was addicted to them. Even so, I loved sharing them, meaning eggs are my "loud made love." Whenever someone visited our home, we made sure they left with a dozen eggs. If we ran low, I hightailed it through the orchard to my father-in-law's back-porch fridge, where he kept the daily stash.

Josiah also wove a spiritual element into this, a double meaning. An egg's center is typically spelled "yolk," but it was no accident when he used "yoke," which was the wooden cross-piece fastened over the necks of two animals and attached to the plow or cart they were to pull. It was his poetic way of pointing to Jesus, who said, "For My yoke is easy and My burden is light."[1]

I almost laughed. Through the words of this autistic boy, the Lord was clearly "yoking" around with me, and this gave me a greater sense of freedom. For years I had endeavored to keep my walk with God fresh, praying and seeking Him on a daily basis. Yes, God's presence was my lifeblood and sustenance, but Josiah reminded me it was in no way an obligation. It was a joy that came from "not worn out yokes." Keeping the relationship fresh each day was essential to living with an awareness of God's forgiveness and love. It was key to overcoming sin and obstacles in my way.

As I moved to the next portion of Josiah's email, my emotions shifted. I realized these words wouldn't make sense to just anyone. To me, though, they were deeply poignant and personal.

He reads big tearful magazines of news.

My wife could verify I had a habit of following sad news stories. I'd wept recently as I read accounts of horrible persecutions going on around the world. Less than twenty-four hours earlier, I had watched a video of a beheading and of Christians lined up one by one and shot. I mourned all day, unable to get those images out of my mind. As a person who felt deeply, I was compelled to agonize over the pain of others, physically and spiritually, groaning in the Spirit. It was a blessing and a curse, which sometimes paralyzed me. I knew I was a unique creation in Christ and chose to believe He had made me just as I was to fulfill His divine purpose—even if it meant lots of tears. Not everyone sought out "tearful magazines of news," as Josiah said, but I did. Josiah, in his unique autistic way, had put that into words.

And he wasn't done describing me:

> Ranging back to his childhood, he very much liked nice daring big questions for daring questions are his holding might. If he knows might, it is nominal compared to knowing right questions to ask of God and people. You like novels, you like ruining doubt.

My emotions shifted again. Alanna and I had a somewhat comical understanding that I would ask her twenty-plus questions a day. It was just who I was and how I interacted with people. Since early childhood I had been a truth seeker and, in Josiah's words, "very much liked nice daring big questions." When I became a Christian, as a teenager, I didn't just believe; I wanted answers to why I believed. Did God really exist? Was Jesus really who He said He was? If so, how could I know? Did God really do miracles today? My questions were endless.

This was OK with God. The Bible states, "You do not have because you do not ask."[2] He wants His people to ask for more of Him, and He is ready to reveal His ways. Another verse says, "You ask and do not receive, because you ask amiss, that you may spend it on your pleasures."[3] I believe it is important "knowing right questions to ask of God," as Josiah said. Ultimately it is about becoming transparent before Him, seeing myself as I really am, broken and in need. As I humble myself and ask Him to reveal His truth, I am desiring the mind of Christ and bringing my requests into alignment with His plans for me.

With all my questions churning inside, it was no accident I

majored in journalism at Ole Miss. True journalism was about asking hard questions and getting to the truth. When my beliefs were challenged in college, I tenaciously sought answers. Eventually, finding the answers to my questions led to the deepest, securest faith. This process was the foundation for my book *The Insanity of Unbelief: A Journalist's Journey From Belief, to Skepticism, to Deep Faith.*

Again, Josiah had nailed it. I certainly did "like ruining doubt."

If my constant questions were a point of humor for my wife, so was my love of food. She ate for nutrition's sake, while I ate like it was an event. I loved playing sports and initially went to Ole Miss on a football scholarship. As a former athlete, even though I ate a lot, I didn't carry a lot of weight, which made Josiah's next comment that much funnier:

> I will say you eat like a big guy but you aren't all that large.

Thank God for that, was all I could think. Well, thank God for that.

———

Leaning back in my seat, I tried to digest all I'd read so far. It seemed like a book's worth of information, though it was really only two pages.

God definitely had my attention. The things He was saying through this nonverbal boy were so on target. What if I wasn't a big hand trained for war? What if I didn't band together worship playlists for sacred times in motels? What if I didn't collect miracle stories? What if I didn't like eggs and just picked at my food instead of devouring it? Who else would know about the nail guns popping at my house or my tears over news stories? Each and every thing was identified correctly. Not one of Josiah's statements was wrong.

Could a stranger just guess all these things about me? Not

unless he was spying on my every move and reading my thoughts. And all of this from a nine-year-old many states away, a boy whose body shook as he tried to type on his keypad.

"Why me?" I wondered. "Why would Max Davis get these incredible words?"

And why through Josiah Cullen?

Both cases, I realized, were acts of God's grace. I was certainly flawed and cracked, with issues, like anyone else. As for Josiah, he couldn't even control all his muscles or bodily functions, yet the Holy Spirit gave him visions unfiltered by common hang-ups and concerns. Josiah simply served as a conduit, dictating what God revealed to him, always pointing to Jesus and never to himself.

And he still had a few things left to say in that January 16 message:

> Make a book to laser in on...the gentle majesty of King Jesus.

I liked that. I couldn't think of a better way to describe the King of the universe, who gave up His heavenly rights, walked the earth as a man, and sacrificed Himself for our sins.

> He is like kingly. Max, Jesus builds. Make no mistake. Manger built for him was sukkah.

Interesting. Josiah wasn't some Hebrew scholar, and even with my biblical training, I had to look up *sukkah*. It is the word for a temporary structure Jews built outside their homes, especially during the festival of Sukkot. It is also used for a livestock barn. Many Jewish scholars maintain that the stable in which Jesus was born was possibly a *sukkah* built for the Feast of Tabernacles.

Josiah continued:

> Temple built for him was a body. Heaven built for him is a Kingdom. Bride built for him is a church.... My bragging is this Jesus is big to my name but I am

    small to deserve his wonderful saving. My name is my
    best made name only because He lives in me.

Yes, Jesus lives in Josiah. That was beautiful. The apostle Paul wrote, "Do you not know yourselves, that Jesus Christ is in you?"[4] Josiah knew this and declared it for himself. This meant as fellow believers, Josiah and I were brothers, though we'd never even met.

Don't you see how amazing all this is? God dwells in us, imperfect vessels, jars of clay, made righteous and precious through Him. He may be King of the universe, but He is not off in some faraway galaxy. He is Immanuel: God with us. He knew I was praying in a motel even when no one else could see. He knew I was connecting my playlists and worshipping Him even when I was all alone in room 120.

He is with you now, this very moment.

He knows the struggles you face and the tears you cry.

If you are a believer, Jesus lives in you—not just in theory but in reality. That makes me your brother. And Josiah too. We all have doubts and questions, fears and temptations. Each of us has a past, and even if we've been forgiven, our old choices still sometimes carry long-term consequences. In the midst of all this, we are family, encouraging, strengthening, and exhorting one another, stirring one another up to do those good works God has planned for us.

Josiah still needs practical help each day, yet God keeps working through him. His messages to me grew even more supernaturally compelling. As you'll see, not one of them was off the mark. That is how God's kingdom works, the least of us being the greatest of all.

It's not always pretty, but it is effective.

It's not always spectacular, but it is supernatural.

Romans 12:2 tells us, "And do not be conformed to this world, but be transformed by the renewing of your mind, that you may prove what is that good and acceptable and perfect will of God."

It is a simple, yet life-transforming, passage. The world has its own system, which is easy to conform to. We live in the world and naturally absorb its ideas and philosophies. It takes no effort to fall in line with its ways of thinking. On the other hand, our minds can be renewed by filling them with the truths of God's Word, speaking scriptures out loud, reminding God and ourselves of His promises, singing His praises, then coming into alignment with those truths.

As you renew your mind each day, something happens. Instead of being conformed, you are transformed. You are empowered and energized.

His peace comes over you.

You mount up with the wings of an eagle.

You walk and do not faint, because you are refreshed and fortified.

You understand God's perfect will for the day and are given grace to see it through.

Make no mistake, this is not positive thinking or mind over matter. It's a very real transformation by God's truth. Getting His Word in us daily is like eating those fresh eggs. We've got to beg Him for this nourishment, feasting on His Word and singing His praises. This is how we renew our minds, revitalize our spirits, and nourish our souls. If we start running low, we must do whatever it takes to reconnect to our source. Being with Him has to become our passion.

7

MORE GREAT NIGHT SESSIONS

Intercession must not be a passing interest; it must become
an ever-growing object of intense desire, for which above
everything we long and live. It is the life of consecration and
self-sacrifice that will indeed give power for intercession.
—ANDREW MURRAY, *GOD'S BEST SECRETS*

February 8, 2015

EXACTLY ONE MONTH after my initial connection with Tahni,
Josiah sent me a third email. I had completed my novel and
turned it in to my publisher, but I was fatigued. We were dealing
with numerous decisions regarding our house under construction, one challenge after another. My faith had skyrocketed after
the first two messages from Josiah, and I braced myself for whatever was next. I wanted nothing more than to know the Lord's
heart and will for me.

This has always been my desire. Since being born again my
junior year of high school, I have dug for answers and sought
God's truth. As a result, I have become a man of prayer.

Even as a teenager, I went on long nature hikes, spending
hours alone with Jesus. A sandy-banked river meandered
through hundreds of acres of forest near my home, and I walked
and talked with Him along the tree-shaded banks, feeling as if
He were right beside me. It was there I first learned to fellowship with God, to meditate on His Word, and to recognize His
voice. This became woven into my DNA. It became a way of life.
Sitting on a log with my feet dangling in the water, I devoured
the truths in my pocket Bible, listening to the Holy Spirit as He
brought illumination. When I prayed, I basically just poured out

my soul as if Jesus were sitting on the log next to me or walking by my side.

I thought this was normal. If Jesus actually lived in me, as Scripture said, then it stood to reason He would speak to my heart.

How could He not?

And how could I not make room each day to hear from Him?

My daily schedule was organized around prayer, and for over thirty-five years, my walks and talks with Jesus had taken me along trails, parks, country roads, rivers, the local high school track—wherever God led. For the past two years, I'd been praying at a nearby basketball court at night. It was a safe and secluded spot outside an abandoned school, where I would walk in circles around the baskets.

Ready now to hear from the Lord, I positioned myself before my computer screen and opened Josiah's latest message. This time it was not only profound but instructional—which seemed about right. In the prophetic realm this was how God often moved, giving a supernatural word to get a person's attention, then following it up with instruction, guidance, rebuke, and/or edification. Well, I had definitely been edified already, and God certainly had my attention.

Josiah started his message:

> Yes. Max Davis, Max Davis. Yes, loudly his name gets
> God's ear. Lining his mine is more gold.

At first, I read over this simple introduction without thinking too much about it. I had God's ear, sure. And a mine was dug to search for gold, gemstones, or other precious metals. What was new? Then I realized there just might be more to this.

I did a little online research and discovered that "lining his mine" was critical to the mining process. *Scientific American* had a whole article titled "Lining Mine Shafts,"[1] and another article on the subject stated, "The shaft lining performs several functions; it is first and foremost a safety feature preventing loose or unstable rock from falling into the shaft."[2] A piece published by the Institute of Physics added, "The state of shaft lining affects not only the safety of people working in it and the transport operations, but also the functioning of the entire mine."[3]

This was all new info to me—but not to God.

It was just remarkable to me that Josiah would know that mines have linings. With this revelation in mind, I pictured myself getting "God's ear," in Josiah's words, through diligent prayer and study of His Word. Digging for His truth, I received "more gold." His golden truths and promises lined, fortified, and protected both me and the work He was doing in me.

Now the message seemed remarkably precise, and I shook my head in awe.

What a word!

It was so easy to live in fear, worrying about the loss of finances or health, careers or relationships. Whole industries revolved around these fears. Self-help books, counselors, insurance agencies, and ministries all tried to ease people's anxieties in a variety of ways. Ultimately, though, my source of peace was God Himself. Jesus was the Prince of Peace. Proverbs 2:3–5 told me, "Yes, if you cry out for discernment, and lift up your voice for understanding, if you seek her as silver, and search for her as for hidden treasures; then you will understand the fear of the LORD, and find the knowledge of God." Hebrews 11:6 also assured me, "He is a rewarder of those who diligently seek Him."

Seeking God and crying out for His truth were like mining for gold. Not only was the gold of His wisdom a reward, but His presence lined and protected me from the crumbling weight of deception and from the onslaughts of life.

Josiah continued:

> Max, is the Mighty One moping over you? No. He is so loudly in love with you....Max, you are Mine from night into day....He knows your days.

These words were more healing than I could explain. Even though I would have never described "the Mighty One moping" over me, I still battled nagging insecurity and feelings that I was stupid and God was disappointed with me. I'd experienced my share of rejection and hurt. Having two great parents didn't prevent me from having a failed first marriage. Going to church didn't mean I never faced people who spouted off ungodly things that reinforced my insecurities and self-hatred. It was confusing at times because I'd hear messages that seemed as if they were from God but didn't line up with His Word. Instead of resting in the secure arms of Jesus' love and letting the Holy Spirit fashion me into His image, I was often driven to simply perform for His acceptance.

Step by step, Jesus' truth was restoring me, shattering these strongholds, and giving me hope. To think that He was "loudly in love" with me "from night into day," as Josiah said, brought this grown man to his knees. It took my breath away. God's love for me was bold and unwavering, even though He knew everything about me—my flaws, my failures, and the skeletons in my closet. Love and grace were part of His nature.

And they weren't just for me but for everyone.

I thought of the apostle Peter. He denied Jesus three times with passionate cursing and swearing, even as soldiers dragged Jesus off to be crucified. Realizing what he'd done, Peter wept bitterly.[4] He felt incredibly unworthy and guilty because he *was* guilty. Days later, after Christ's resurrection and before His ascension, Peter was fishing on his boat when he saw Jesus along the lakeshore. He jumped into the water and swam to Him. There, Jesus asked Peter three times if he loved Him. "The third time he said to him, 'Simon son of John, do you love me?' Peter was hurt because Jesus asked him the third time, 'Do you love me?' He said, 'Lord, you know all things; you know that I love you.' Jesus said, 'Feed my sheep.'"[5]

Jesus knew Peter loved Him. Jesus also knew it was possible

for people to love Him deeply and still fail Him miserably. Once Peter's heart was set right again, Jesus told His disciple, "Feed my sheep."

Grace forgives you and then gives you an assignment. How incredible is that? Jesus wants to be in relationship with His people, and from that relationship flow their assignments. "You are Mine," He was reminding me, as Josiah said. Not only did I have a relationship with Him, but I could trust Him to dig up the gold in me while lining and protecting the whole operation.

"You don't have to worry, Max," I told myself. Jesus "knows your days," as Josiah said. Day by day, you can surrender the treasures of your heart to Him.

———

Of course, Josiah wasn't done:

> Think grace and you will get grace. Think holy and you will get holy. Think holy grace and you will get holy grace.

Grace and holiness went together. That was biblically correct. The following scriptures summed them up perfectly.

- **Grace**: "Not by works of righteousness which we have done, but according to His mercy He saved us, through the washing of regeneration and renewing of the Holy Spirit, whom He poured out on us abundantly through Jesus Christ our Savior, that having been justified by His grace we should become heirs according to the hope of eternal life" (Titus 3:5–7).

- **Holiness**: "For the grace of God that brings salvation has appeared to all men, teaching us that, denying ungodliness and worldly lusts, we should live soberly, righteously, and godly in the present age, looking for the blessed hope and glorious appearing of our great God and Savior Jesus Christ, who gave Himself for us, that He might redeem us from every lawless deed and purify for Himself His own special people, zealous for good works" (Titus 2:11–14).

As Christians, we are saved by grace alone, and that is our foundation. That grace, however, leads us into holiness. Just as Josiah said, it is "holy grace." I couldn't think of a better way to wrap up his words of edification and encouragement.

I was now ready for the prophetic instruction, which came next:

Make more great night sessions. Yes, more night intercessions. You trial for your bright home that is getting built, but you need more night sessions in intercession for your maybes to become yeses, Max. Joy comes in the morning by praying in the night. Pray more at night by making time for intercession.

A whole book could be written on just that paragraph. There was so much to unravel. It was true, Alanna and I were facing a number of trials with our "bright home…getting built." We had so many things to figure out, and the arrow on my stress meter was pointed into bright red!

Everything I'd gotten from Josiah up to that point had been God showing me He knew exactly where I was and what I was up to. Now He was confirming for me the importance of intercessory prayer. With all we had going on in the Davis household, in the midst of the turmoil, I needed to "make more great night sessions…more night intercessions," as Josiah said.

The Holy Spirit was wooing me. Through this precious autistic boy, He was calling me to spend more time with Jesus.

And He's calling you too, even right now. He loves you more

than you know. Even as you read this, He wants you to know the grace and the assignment He has for you.

If you think I'm someone special, I'm not. My hope rests totally and completely in what Jesus did for me at the cross. Receiving all these words and encounters was not because I'm all that but rather *despite* all that. They were sent individually to me, yet even as they arrived, I knew they were meant to be shared with others. As a result, I started a series on social media called *#HopeIsAPerson*, and the response has been overwhelming. People are desperate for hope. One pastor was so touched by the posts, he wrote a song about them. His lyrics depict how I and a lot of other folks feel:

> When I look in the mirror, sometimes I don't like
> what I see.
> There's pain in the eyes of the man looking back at
> me...
> As I think about it, I can clearly see, my pain has
> been caused by others;
> my pain has been caused by me.
> But Hope is a person.

That person is Jesus. To move into the depths with God and walk in awareness of His presence, we must be convinced beyond a shadow of a doubt that He loves us, and not only that He loves us but that He's crazy in love with us. We all have someone we love so much we'd give our lives for them. Thankfully most of us never have to do so. Well, God loves you that deeply and even more. He didn't choose to give just His life for you—He gave His Son's life for you!

God's love draws us into His presence. It's a divine romance. "How much more," wrote the apostle Paul, "will those who receive God's abundant provision of grace and of the gift of righteousness reign in life through the one man, Jesus Christ!"[6] If you've received His provision of grace and gift of righteousness, you are one with Him and have the Holy Spirit in you.

God is not disappointed in you. That is a lie from the deceiver!

He doesn't feel listless apathy toward you—another lie!

In fact, He is delighted you are trusting Him by faith. He wants to free you from the sins and strongholds that bind you. The apostle John wrote, "He who believes in Him is not condemned."[7] And Psalm 147:11 says, "The LORD takes pleasure in those who fear Him, in those who hope in His mercy." Do you see that? You are not condemned but celebrated. "The LORD your God is in your midst, a mighty one who will save; he will rejoice over you with gladness; he will quiet you by his love; he will exult over you with loud singing."[8]

Once again, Josiah's message nailed it. The first step to experiencing God's best for you is to be secure in His love and cling to His promises. God rejoices over you just as you are, flaws and all. He's not "moping over you," as Josiah said. He's "loudly in love" with you. Imagine that!

8

SITTING IN THE FREEDOM OF JESUS

Your own secret place is where you, like David, can "behold the beauty of the Lord," enjoying your unique experience of God as He reveals Himself to you with an intimacy that brings more inner satisfaction than anything else possibly could.
—J. Otis Ledbetter, *In the Secret Place*

February 9, 2015

THE CALL WAS clear. God wanted me to spend more time crying out to Him and listening for His voice.

Our forty acres of family land has a narrow limestone road and foot trails that weave their way through the trees and around a couple of fields. That week the south Louisiana weather was crisp and cool, with temperatures in the midforties and fifties at night. As soon as Alanna began preparing for bed, I zipped up my jacket and headed into the woods to meet with Jesus. It was dark and shadowy back there, but my usual night prayer spot at the basketball court was being bulldozed. The woods would have to do.

Only a day had passed since the third message from Josiah, and I knew God didn't do supernatural things like this frivolously. I was answering the call from the Holy Spirit to "have more night intercessions," in Josiah's words. All that was needed was to show up with an expectant heart.

And I *was* expectant. I *wanted* to do this.

I knew this call wasn't an issue of my faith, my salvation by grace alone, or my doing some religious works to make myself more acceptable to God. I was already accepted through my faith, and I trusted in His promises. It wasn't even about my

46

regular times of Bible study, contemplation, church attendance, and prayer—all of which were critical to the Christian life. I was already a man of intense prayer who'd walked with God for years, and I knew His reality. We had experienced much together, even several supernatural experiences. I felt securely grounded in Scripture and was unmoved by strange doctrines or feelings. The Holy Spirit was in me and sealed me as a son of the Most High.

No, it wasn't about any of that. It was about me pressing through the distractions, pain, and pulls of life into God's presence. Only there could I truly hear.

I realize, of course, people can't always spend uninterrupted hours with the Lord. However, the Holy Spirit can reveal Himself whenever we take advantage of the time available to us. It is about shifting focus to hear God's voice. My own fellowship with Jesus has looked different at different seasons in my life, but I know His presence can be experienced anywhere, anytime—perhaps on a short walk, in the car, or on the lawn mower. God often speaks to me while I am driving my tractor.

Once, I had a God encounter during an unexpected and frustrating layover at an airport. After walking around the terminal for a long while, bored out of my mind, I noticed the chapel sign. I went in and sat quietly before the Lord with His Word. There was a little book on the altar where people could leave prayer requests. I started thumbing through it, reading the requests, and was quickly reminded that a lot of people were going through much more serious and painful situations. As I prayed for them, the presence of Jesus descended on me, filling me with peace and renewal. My circumstances of being stuck in a layover didn't change, but my heart changed.

Simply put, I was driving into the woods because Jesus wanted us to spend more time together so He could pour more of Himself into me. This was an intimate relationship between the two of us. And He was about to teach me one of the greatest lessons of my life and ministry.

For the next few nights, I sensed His presence as I danced between the timbers underneath a canopy of stars and moonlight, sometimes into the wee hours of the morning. I worshipped God in harmony with the trees as they clapped their hands and the wind rustled through their leaves. There were shouts of praise and proclamations of the Scripture written on my heart. We talked. There was stillness and quiet listening, an occasional owl hooting.

And there were tears—tears of repentance of my own unworthiness, tears of gratitude for His love and grace, tears of joy.

Then there were hugs—a Father embracing His son, a son embracing his Father.

I found this perfect spot back in the woods where two gigantic oak trees grew several yards apart. I paced round and round those trees, crying out and worshipping, praying in the Spirit. A short distance away, there was a small garden shed with a wooden porch swing. My brother-in-law had taken some wood from our old house that was torn down and built the shed back there. It had only been there a month or so. With no electricity, it was one lone structure smack-dab in the middle of the forty-acre woods. It was a perfect place to rest and meditate.

As a man of routine, here is what I did each night beneath the stars. For an hour or so, I cried out to Jesus while circling those two trees—the tears. At some point during this time, His peace descended and wrapped around me like a blanket—the hugs. For a while, the praise and worship just intensified. Then a stillness and quietness followed, during which I sat on the porch swing, basking in a tangible manifestation of His presence.

This wasn't some new age visualization but an amplified awareness that Jesus, the Creator of the universe, was in my midst. Of course, His Spirit was already inside me whether I felt it or not, but this was as if He were sitting right next to me, overwhelming me with His love. It wasn't some emotion I manufactured. It was real. The warm oil of the Holy Spirit poured over me as wave after wave of His peace washed through the core of my being. A sense of wholeness, satisfaction, and indescribable rest filled me—all while I sat in the swing, in the middle of the woods, in the middle of the night.

Time seemed to stop.

I could have stayed in that moment forever.

Eventually the outward manifestation lifted, but I carried with me a fresh awareness that the living Jesus was indeed inside me. Oh, I still had unresolved issues and struggles and painful situations I wrestled with, yet my heart brimmed with His "peace that passes all understanding."[1]

Here was the great lesson I learned: out of my intimacy with Jesus flowed everything else that mattered in my life, from how to love my wife to writing words on a page to understanding His will for daily situations. The key to living a life of impact was the anointing, and the anointing came as a result of being tuned in to His voice and moving in the flow of the Holy Spirit.

———

February 12, 2015

Three nights in a row I had visited my spot in the woods, and that morning my heart was still skipping like a love-smitten teenager's. I was so anxious to get back into Jesus' presence. Before my day got started, I checked my cell phone and noticed a new email from Josiah Cullen.

Another one? Only four days after the last? Now I just felt spoiled.

Heart beating, I opened the message, and my eyes could hardly believe what they were reading.

> Might Max get big nights turned to his very good advantage?...He sat in the freedom of Jesus for nights at a very great night time...in the very nice woods.... He must be going to your night prayer; you made an altar for Him there....This call today is creating freedom in you. Jesus felt a very big hello from your view.

Whoa. The things this boy knew!

How many people actually went to pray in the woods in the middle of the night and sat while experiencing the presence of Jesus? Not my usual spot, either. Yet that's exactly where I'd been the past few evenings, and absolutely no one but my wife knew this. I rarely, if ever, went out in our woods after dark. My only reasons for praying there recently had been the perfect weather, the new garden shed, and the fact that the basketball court was gone. And until this week, I had never sat in the porch swing past sunset.

Tears welled up in me as I read the message again. This was too much. It was more than some random guesswork. God was prophetically using this autistic boy in Minnesota to assure me He'd seen me these past "big nights" as I sat in that swing, "in the freedom of Jesus," out there "in the very nice woods." At my spot between those two trees and in the swing, I'd "made an altar for Him." He really *was* present. It wasn't just some emotional fabrication of mine.

The whole experience reminded me of the story recorded in John 1:43–51, when Jesus saw Nathanael coming toward him and said, "Behold, an Israelite indeed, in whom is no deceit!" (v. 47).

Nathanael asked, "How do You know me?" (v. 48).

Jesus answered, "Before Philip called you, when you were under the fig tree, I saw you" (v. 48).

Nathanael responded, "Rabbi, You are the Son of God! You are the King of Israel!" (v. 49).

The reason Nathanael got so excited was he knew Jesus hadn't been there to see him under that tree, not in the natural realm. Most scholars believe Nathanael had been praying in a private location, as was the custom of Jews in that day. Some contend he was in deep intercession, longing for the coming Messiah. At any rate, that particular fig tree was an important spot for him, a sacred place of communion. It was likely he had encountered God there, like I had in that porch swing at night.

Charles Spurgeon wrote:

> He [Nathanael] had looked around the garden, and fastened the gate so that no one might come in, and he had poured into the ear of his God some very tender confession, under the shade of the fig tree. When Christ said to him, "When you were under the fig tree," it brought to his memory how he poured out his broken and his contrite spirit, and confessed sins unknown to all except God....Or under the fig tree he had been engaged in *very earnest prayer.* Was that fig tree to Nathanael what Peniel was to Jacob, a place where he had wrestled until the break of day, pleading with God?...Once more, it may be that under that fig tree he had enjoyed the sweetest *communion* with his God.[2]

What if Nathanael hadn't spent time under the fig tree? Jesus' words would have made no sense. What if I hadn't prayed in the woods in the middle of the night and encountered the Lord's presence while sitting in the swing? Josiah's words would have made no sense.

But they did make sense. This was supernatural.

It was God.

My response to Josiah's email was similar to Nathanael's: "Jesus, You really are alive and fully present! You see me when I pray!"

9

TWO LOCKS INSTALLED

Sometimes at that moment a wave of light breaks
into our darkness, and it is as though a voice
were saying: "You are accepted. You are accepted,
accepted by that which is greater than you."
—Paul Tillich, *The Shaking of the Foundations*

February 12, 2015

THIS LATEST MESSAGE from Josiah continued for over two pages, crammed with further information about things only my wife and I were aware of. Through this young boy, God was giving me dumbfounding insights and wisdom about how to move forward in ministry. I would never be the same. How could my life not be changed forever? I was reminded once again, there are no limits on what God can do or whom He can do it through. I thanked Him for His incredible grace.

Grace is huge in my life, really huge.

As I alluded to earlier, I came out of an extremely law-based, hyper-legalistic religious background. Since childhood I had struggled with feelings that God was mad at me, at best He was disappointed with me. My personal failures only added to the feelings of shame. When I finally heard the message of grace—that Jesus' righteousness was imputed to me by faith, not through works—it revolutionized my life. For over two decades I sat under some of the most prolific grace teachers in the world.

The message of grace is ingrained in me like my miracle stories. If you are around me to hear about my collection of miracle stories, you will also hear about grace. My life verse is 2 Corinthians 12:9: "My grace is sufficient for you."

Bottom line: If God wanted to speak through a boy who couldn't even use the bathroom without help, who was I to question it? His Word told me He opposed the proud but gave grace to the humble.[1]

Please, Lord, give me more. You know I eat like a big guy—and I'm hungry!

Well, there was plenty more in Josiah's email.

> Reasonable rivers are great in the very nice woods. But reasonable rivers create tributaries with their power. Reasonable rivers need dual locks and gates to be great and mighty. Tell Max that freedom is the day he gets 2 locks installed into his flow. Two locks, two locks, two locks…get built into your river two locks.

There was a lot there, but it wasn't all clear at first. I had to sit back and let the words sink in. Sure, I knew where the "very nice woods" were and that there was a beautiful winding river less than a mile as the crow flies from my home, but was I the "reasonable rivers" Josiah was referring to? Or was this a reference to my prayers? And did "rivers create tributaries," or was it the other way around? I wasn't certain about the "locks and gates" either, but "two locks" were emphasized over and over. They had to be important.

Josiah seemed to anticipate my questions:

> Might they be known already? Like big nights in motels, you gave big locks to God. Might you nightly make intercession one lock.

I was familiar with locks. In Louisiana massive engineering locks were built decades ago to harness the mighty waters of the Mississippi River. When maintained and used properly, the locks play a huge role in diverting disaster. We need everything the river has to offer for our livelihoods, but it has to be channeled correctly. Locks are also used to direct ships and move them from one level up to the next. As a lock opens, water flows in and lifts the ship—a water elevator, as some call it.

Lord, what did it all mean?

That's when I realized the key to understanding all this was in John 7:37–39, where Jesus said, "'If anyone is thirsty, let him come to Me and drink. He who believes in Me, as the Scripture said, 'From his innermost being will flow rivers of living water.' But this He spoke of the Spirit, whom those who believed in Him were to receive.'"

The Holy Spirit—He was the *rivers of living water*, the "reasonable rivers"!

Again, Josiah's message showed pinpoint biblical accuracy. His application of these theological truths was beyond that of many scholars, and now I had the whole picture. It was incredible.

Each night, God's Spirit was flowing, as Josiah said, with "great" energy "in the very nice woods" as I did intercessory warfare. Yes, He could "create tributaries," and He did, by branching out through me to others. As believers we are all ships being guided and directed along mighty waters. When we enter a lock in intercession, the Holy Spirit lifts us to the next level. When we turn to God in prayer and intimacy, He moves us to even higher levels, navigating us beyond our circumstances and enabling us to flow in the "freedom" of His Spirit.

Josiah's message was so encouraging and challenging. I loved it. When he said, "Freedom is the day he gets 2 locks installed into his flow," I already knew what my first lock was. For years I had endeavored to "nightly make intercession," and it was incredibly affirming to know my prayers were being heard. I wasn't crying out to a God who cannot hear or spilling tears to a God who doesn't care. He is alive and present and active!

A major part of my intercession is praying for others. After reading the Word, worshipping, and praying in the Spirit, I couldn't pray for myself until I had finished talking to God about my peeps—the people I regularly brought before Him and those He directed me to intercede for that day. As I was in intimate fellowship with the Holy Spirit, in the flow of His river, He brought individuals to my mind, often giving me personal words for them. He promised me if I cried out to Him on others' behalf, He would supernaturally take care of me.

Colossians 4:12 gives a specific example of intercession when it says, "Epaphras, who is one of you and a servant of Christ Jesus, sends greetings. He is always wrestling in prayer for you, that you may stand firm in all the will of God, mature and fully assured" (NIV). God promises in Psalm 32:8, "I will instruct you and teach you in the way you should go; I will guide you with My eye." And in Jeremiah 33:3 He urges, "Call to me and I will answer you and tell you great and unsearchable things you do not know" (NIV).

I found so much freedom sitting in the Lord's presence. When I was in the flow of His Spirit, that fresh, living water made my work less of an effort. It carried me along in His current. I'd heard it preached, "The key to success in our lives is to find where the Holy Spirit is flowing and jump in!" I agree. One writer called this "living at the pace of grace." Or it could be called "living in the flow." Both sound like winners to me!

Josiah mentioned "2 locks installed," though. "Two locks, two locks, two locks..."

I vividly recalled several "big nights in motels" when I interceded and gave my "big locks," writing and ministry, to the Lord. In that motel room, I placed my writing on the altar and said, "God, You can have it. Unless You do it, I want no part in it. Direct me, Lord. Show me. I don't want to write a single word unless it's from You. If You want me to do something else, I will. I'll walk away right now if that is what You want."

Was writing the second lock? No, that just didn't seem to fit.

I read more from Josiah:

> Loud very big nice verse is biting my reality. It is
> very large to your life. This verse is very big to night

intercession for you. It says this. My grace is sufficient
for you.

The words jumped out at me. I couldn't make this stuff up.
Of all the scriptures Josiah might have labored away to spell out
with one shaky finger, he chose 2 Corinthians 12:9. He could
have come up with something that had no personal meaning to
me, but he didn't. No; he chose my *life verse!* My sweet daughter-
in-law would even burn those words onto a wooden plaque for
my office, just as they were burned onto my heart!

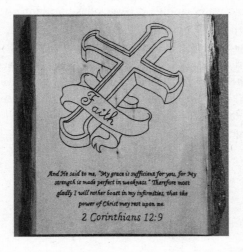

*And He said to me, "My grace is sufficient for you, for My
strength is made perfect in weakness." Therefore most
gladly I will rather boast in my infirmities, that the
power of Christ may rest upon me.*
2 Corinthians 12:9

Josiah wasn't kidding about this "big nice verse" being "very
large" to my life and "very big" to my evenings of intercession.
Grace is critical. Grace makes intercession possible. On the
cross, Jesus bridged the gap between heaven and earth. He paid
the price for the sin that separated us from God. He wants us
to follow His example and stand in the gap for others, taking
advantage of what He made possible, declaring the freedom He
bought with His blood. By His grace we enter into His presence
and bask in His love—two locks, grace and intercession.

These "dual locks" harness and release the river's "great and mighty" power. They work together, directing ships and lifting them up to new horizons. From my writing to my relationships, everything else flows when I keep these two locks as my priority.

Whew! It was a lot to absorb. So many insights and things to consider.

Maybe you feel the same way after reading these pages. Maybe you need to stick a bookmark right here, take a walk outside, and thank the Lord for His grace in your own life. We're not done, though. Not even close. The river of the Holy Spirit is much deeper, wider, and purer than the Mississippi. It's an everlasting flow of living water, and God always has more for us.

He certainly did for me.

Tahni had asked me to let her know if I didn't understand something her son sent, or if something was off or incorrect. She wanted to help him learn to discern what he heard from the Holy Spirit. Well, so far he'd been right on the mark, and as you'll see, my encounters with him continued to get even more supernaturally accurate!

10

POPPING TO PAPA

*Before I try to attempt anything for God, I've got to come
out of His presence. I've got to come out with something that
I've received in His presence that is changing me. I have been
changed. I have not gotten this in a seminary. I have not gotten
this from man. I got this alone with Jesus, beholding His face.*
—DAVID WILKERSON

February 18, 2015

MID-MONTH A SEVERE rainy season set in. I'm talking days
and days of solid downpours. Praying at night in the
woods was over. Praying anywhere outside was over unless I went
to the motel on the coast. I had to come up with another option.

At that point, our house under construction was almost
done—a roof in place, drywall hung on the walls, bare plywood
floors, windows and doors, but no electricity. I grabbed my LED
flashlight and sloshed across our property toward the site. Maybe
I could pray over there.

After that first night, I ran back to the trailer, huffing and
puffing. "Alanna," I called out, "I found a new place to pray; I
found a new place to pray! It's in the house!"

I was so pumped. Some people get excited about their new
man cave, pantry, or sundeck, and there is nothing wrong with
those things. I just get really excited about locations for intercession. Soon I would have my own wonderful new office to write
in, and I was already consecrating it as a place of prayer before it
was even completed!

Nightly I went over with my little flashlight. I stuck it in
the doorknob hole to have some light as I paced in circles,

worshipping God, crying out to Him, and praying in the Spirit. Yes, I was speaking in my prayer language.[1] Intercessory prayer in the house at night became my *passion*. I couldn't wait! I longed for it, craved it. My favorite thing was to be in God's presence with no distractions, shut away with Him.

Out in nature was a great place to hear from the Lord, but I also found myself noticing the beauty all around. There was something profound about blocking everything else out and focusing totally on Jesus, intensely crying out to Him. Praying in the woods at night was like that. With the darkness blocking out distractions, I could press through to another level—not another level of some spiritual supremacy or acceptance but into Him. When I did, something special happened.

The house became my new secret place. My previous intensity in prayer at the motels and my freedom in the woods shifted to our new home. It occurred nightly. It was amazing!

March 12, 2015

A couple of weeks into my praying at the house, I received a sovereign message from Josiah. *Sovereign* was the only word for it, because this download came to him all of a sudden, with no outside prompting or communication, while he was in the middle of something else. As usual, he pecked the letters into his tablet, and Tahni forwarded it to me with this brief explanation: "Hi, Max! Wow, Josiah was totally in the middle of a different topic and different sentence and suddenly this came."

I read the latest from her boy, imagining his blue eyes roving the keypad while he groaned and jerked and tried to get everything down. My own doubts were long gone, and I just felt honored to get these words from the Lord through one of His earthen vessels.

They read:

Pop pop pop. Lots of popping…Loud popping is very
loud to my ears. Pop pop pop, Mom. Loud big house
is popping to papa papa papa. Mom, my popping is
just intense. Past loud popping was nails but loud
popping now is papa papa papa. Max nightly papas.
Joy is his prayers to papa.

Whaaaat? I was flabbergasted. Come on now!

Like Josiah said, the "past loud popping was nails," but with
that construction phase over, the "big house" was making a different sound. What he heard was "just intense." It wasn't the
single-shot firing of the nail guns. This sound was more of a
semiautomatic burst. The "loud popping is papa papa papa." I
knew exactly what he was hearing, and he got it absolutely right.
The manual labor was done, and now spiritual warfare was hap-
pening beneath that roof. The house was "popping to papa papa
papa" as I cried out to my heavenly Papa. In the straightforward
words of an autistic boy, "Max nightly papas."

How could anyone second-guess the Lord's hand in this? No
one, and I mean *no one*, knew I was praying in that house except
Alanna. It hadn't even been an option for me a few months earlier because it was just being built and I could only pray there at
night because of workers on site during the day.

The next day, I sent Tahni a text message that said, "What
nobody knows is I started praying in the house at night a couple
weeks ago."

God was letting Josiah hear my nightly prayers at the house.

And they weren't just bouncing off the walls. They were "very
loud"!

Nothing brought me more "joy" than my "prayers to papa."

Tears welled in my eyes as I read these incredibly confirming
words from the Lord. There were moments the enemy tried
telling me I was wasting my time, I was doing it wrong, and I
wasn't worthy. He threw painful memories in my face—the
legalistic religion of my childhood, the glaring rebellion of my

teenage years, my previous failed marriage, and some poor decisions I had made that hurt people. Well, none of those mattered. Who cared about the lies of a deceiver and the mistakes of the past when the Lord of creation was in the house!

Josiah went on:

> Joy is his prayers to papa. Max builds papa up. Max builds nights to papa's heart. Max needs holy hello. Max bites his named inheritance of lovely papaing. Max gets very hopeful in his very papaing. Max needs papa. Papa loves Max to need him so.

I felt every bit of that "holy hello," and my heart was ready to burst. What could I say?

When Josiah mentioned, "Max bites his named inheritance," it sounded kind of funny, but I knew it was profound. According to the dictionary, to bite is "to cut, wound, or tear with the teeth"; "to grip or hold with teeth."[2] It is synonymous with the phrase *sink one's teeth into.*[3] The picture was pretty obvious. As one of Papa's kids, I had an inheritance worth sinking my teeth into. It was mine, and no one could take it away. Earlier in life I had tried finding love and acceptance in plenty of other ways and been mired in hopelessness. It was God's love and grace that pulled me out. What could be better than a "named inheritance of lovely papaing"?

Another picture came to mind, adding even deeper layers of beauty—my grandchildren! Nobody warned Alanna and me about grandchildren. They just swooped in and stole our hearts. We are Nana and Papa to them, and when they come over, everything else stops. We drop whatever we are doing to be with them. We often just set them in the middle of the floor and watch for hours as they do whatever they do. They are the prettiest, smartest, and sweetest. We take pictures—and all our Facebook friends know it!

As our grandchildren have grown, they have learned that

Papa's house is their house. They have full authority here. They also know Papa has treats. When they come over, they make a mad dash to the fridge and jerk that thing open with shameless boldness to pull out those goodies! I'm talking ice cream bars, yogurt with candies, ice pops. Then they make their way to the pantry for cookies and whatever else they can find. They have full permission. What is mine is theirs. I put all those treats there just for them, and if they don't go after them, I get a little sad. But when they find them, I just want to burst with joy! Very often they crawl up into our laps afterward, and we all sit there together, content as ever.

This is what Papa God wants. He wants us to take full advantage of our inheritance. The Book of Hebrews says, "Let us therefore come boldly to the throne of grace, that we may obtain mercy and find grace to help in time of need....Therefore, brethren, having boldness to enter the Holiest by the blood of Jesus, by a new and living way which He consecrated for us, through the veil, that is, His flesh, and having a High Priest over the house of God, let us draw near with a true heart in full assurance of faith."[4]

My Christianity, my faith, my prayers aren't about me trying to please some angry, distant God. They are my connection through the blood of Jesus and the seal of the Holy Spirit to Papa God. Because of what Jesus did on the cross, we can approach our heavenly Father with shameless boldness and full assurance of His love. He has made a way for us to raid His fridge and crawl up into His lap. This gives Him great joy!

So many of God's kids aren't sinking "bites" into their "named inheritance." They are tiptoeing around in fear that He'll whack them, but that isn't His nature. He is a good, good Father. We can enter His presence with childlike faith and wonder. He is just longing for us to crawl up into His lap and get some hugs!

This was so good I couldn't wait for more.

11

THE MOST POWERFUL
PLACE WE CAN EVER BE

*Abiding is all about the most important friendship of your
life. Abiding doesn't measure how much you know about
your faith or your Bible. In abiding, you seek, long for, thirst
for, wait for, see, know, love, hear, and respond to a person.*
—Bruce Wilkinson, *Secrets of the Vine*

March 12, 2015

JOSIAH'S NEXT WORDS from the same message were equally as
insightful and on-target:

> Max is arguing loudly in the spirit for daily jails to
> break open. Wait, mom I have more. Holy holy holy
> is The Lord God Almighty who was and is and is to
> come. Max, you get big into holiness. Loudly build lap
> up to sit in father's lap, Max. Great faith is Max's very
> big passion for loud papaing. Hearing big papaing is
> very nightly fantastic to papa.

Others could believe what they wanted, but I knew this was
supernatural. Without any contact or knowledge from me, a boy
in Minnesota was seeing and hearing my evening prayers in that
house.

I was absolutely "arguing loudly in the spirit," walking in
circles, calling out in my prayer language. I was warring for
"daily jails to break open." I was also resting in God's presence.
Each night, I would grab my Bible, "loudly build lap up to sit in
father's lap," and let Him share from His Book with me. When

I did, something wonderful and supernatural occurred. I wasn't praying to get something, though petition was an important part of praying, but just relaxing in His arms, beholding His face, abiding in His presence. That's what moved the heart of God, because "Papa loves Max to need him so." And as much as I loved being with Him, it was "very nightly fantastic to Papa."

Josiah's message carried on, and each word was significant.

> Making hours in intercession's goal is announcing daring books but also announcing holy saturation of salivating over entirely panting for papa. Max, you need more boasting than ever in he who pens your loud artful papa book.

I was in tears all over again. The time I spend seeking the Holy Spirit's flow is one of my locks, giving direction and power to my assignments. If I'm not "making hours in intercession," there is no reason to be "announcing daring books." I want each book to honor the Lord. It is all about Him. I can't do anything in life without Him.

A powerful man of God once told me, "Max, the greatest challenge a man or woman of prayer will ever face is learning to spend time with God and pray without an agenda other than to know Him and listen." Even though my writing and books are an important assignment, my first priority is "holy saturation." My heavenly Father wants to fill me completely with His Spirit. He covets our times together and loves for me to depend on Him.

"As the deer pants for streams of water," David penned in Psalm 42, "so my soul pants for you, my God."[1] That isn't just some feel-good poem or song but the sort of deep yearning God desires. On the run from his enemies, David was panting for God because he was physically exhausted, spiritually frustrated, and emotionally broken. According to scholars, the image portrayed here is one not just of desire but of desperation. The deer was weary and worn from evading predators and the scorching sun. In the distance, it saw a stream and panted, longing to lap up the cool, refreshing spring waters to replenish its parched body and mind.

David craved God in the same way. He was foreshadowing what Jesus told the woman at the well when He said, "Whoever drinks the water I give them will never thirst. Indeed, the water I give them will become in them a spring of water welling up to eternal life."[2] David understood where his strength came from. Being in God's presence sustained him, whether he was on a hillside tending sheep as a young shepherd, in a cave as a mighty warrior on the run, or in the palace temple ruling as the king of Israel.

From his autistic mind, Josiah depicted a picture remarkably close to David's psalm, and it resonated with me. I was desperate every day for the living water, "salivating" and "entirely panting for papa." Anytime I tried something else to slake my thirst, it was temporary and often contaminated. Only living water could satisfy. Only He could sustain and refresh me when I was parched and weary and the world was falling apart around me. Unless I was filled with God's Spirit, He couldn't pen "loud, artful" words through me.

This urgent cry from the heart is something I call "desperate dependence." I even wrote a book with that title. Desperate dependence is reaching that place in life where God truly becomes our source for everything. Getting to that place requires coming to the end of ourselves and crying out to Him. C. S. Lewis explained in his book *Mere Christianity* that until we come to the point in life of "throwing in the sponge" and saying, "You must do this; I can't," God can't "get down to business with us."[3] We rarely reach that point voluntarily because it is uncomfortable and usually painful, but when we do, His best for us can truly begin.

I was overwhelmed again by all these revelations in a simple email. As the wind blew through the oak trees outside and as

Alanna prepared a meal in our mobile-home kitchen, I came to the end of Josiah's message:

> Papa is not grand to most people because they never hire their notice of him in their lives. Father God tells me only when joy meets papaing he dares to send his love like this. Max, you get joyful in papaing. Max, you get big in holiness....Max, you pair up joy with papaing. Joy is big to father's ears. Joy, more love, is more papas in your loud loud loud house....Might you look at papa mightily? Only papa is looking to let you know papa is looking at you too. Max, noting big finishing of mighty popping....Love, Josiah.

I read this section again and noticed *joy* used five times: "joy meets papaing," "joyful in papaing," "joy with papaing," "joy is big to father's ears," and "joy, more love, is more papas." Each instance was connected to spending time with God. Looking back, in the places I had prayed and also received messages from Josiah—the motel, the woods, the unfinished house—I'd desired God's presence more than anything else. It wasn't out of some religious duty or ritual. It was out of joy, out of pure childlike anticipation.

And in the midst of that joy, He dared "to send his love."

In other words, Papa showed up with hugs!

He loves all His children unconditionally, of course, but the ones sitting in His lap get the hugs. I thought of my own grand-babies, how they love to climb up and sit in Nana's and Papa's laps. I love those intimate, spontaneous moments. Time stops and the joy is indescribable. This is exactly what our heavenly Father desires with us, not some dry religious ritual.

It reminded me of something I read in John Piper's book *Desiring God*:

> For many, Christianity has become the grinding out
> of general doctrinal laws from collections of biblical

facts. But childlike wonder and awe have died. The scenery and poetry and music of the majesty of God have dried up like a forgotten peach at the back of the refrigerator.[4]

God isn't far away and uninvolved in our lives. He wants relationship, connection, interaction. That was what Josiah meant when he wrote, "You look at papa mightily....Papa is looking at you too." The Lord was saying joy is a two-way street. My prayers give Him great joy, and His presence gives me great joy. It was indescribable! It was as if God were peeling back the layers of heaven so I could see what my prayers looked like from His point of view.

As a fun final note, Josiah mentioned a "big finishing of mighty popping." Since I already knew "popping" was our construction and "papaing" was my praying, I realized he was envisioning our house nearly complete in the trim-out phrase. He had never seen our place in person or in pictures, but it was revealed to him by God's Spirit exactly where it was in the process. The Lord was saying He cared about my prayers and spiritual endeavors—and my earthly endeavors too.

"C'mon, now," I thought. "How cool is that?"

———

Let me say again, I am no one special. God shared these words with me through Josiah so I could share them with you. Feel free to share them with others you know.

If you're like me, you'd love a little joy in the midst of everything life throws at us. Well, what about a big ole helping of it? That's what Josiah's message was all about, offering a clear understanding of joy found by basking in God's incredible love, acceptance, and peace.

Do you want to be truly transformed?

Run to Him. Pant after Him. Salivate for His presence.

I'm not saying to add another chore to your spiritual checklist. God is tossing aside the lists and inviting you to burst through the front doors, raid the refrigerator, and crawl up into His lap! He wants you to live in spiritual awareness of His presence, knowing He is real and alive. This creates an expectancy, a passion, a joy. It's the joy Josiah mentioned five times. Do you think maybe it's important to your Papa?

In Psalm 16:11, David said, "In Your presence is fullness of joy." Obviously, in heaven we will experience unspeakable, unimaginable joy because we will be freed from our sin natures and forever in God's presence. Yet we can experience a portion of that joy and peace here on earth. That's what David was talking about. And that joy is a key to life.

Are you getting this? You *can* have joy in the midst of horrendous circumstances. Joy is *not* just happiness or the absence of pain.

"Do not sorrow," Nehemiah declared, "for the joy of the LORD is your strength."[5] What an amazing statement, considering the circumstances at that time. Jerusalem's city walls were in utter disrepair, and invaders were at their doorstep. The people were living in dire situations, facing poverty and violence. They were fighting for their families—their wives, sons, daughters, and homes.[6] Describing the time of Nehemiah, author Anne McCain wrote, "A city lacking a strong surrounding wall was subject to all kinds of terrors. It was vulnerable to attack by any number of enemies. Invaders could do harm both to people and to crops and gardens. A broken-down wall meant a physically and economically unstable environment."[7]

Yet Nehemiah tells them their strength is in the joy of the Lord!

Think about it. If there's fullness of joy in His presence and His joy is our strength, then we know where to go for our ultimate power in life. God's presence gives us joy, which gives us strength. Don't seek experiences; seek Him. Just sit in His lap.

When you do, He sends His love and stuff happens. The most powerful place we can ever be is in God's presence.

"These things I have spoken to you," Jesus said, "that My joy may remain in you, and that your joy may be full."[8]

"The presence of Jesus, distinctly manifested, cannot but give joy," Andrew Murray wrote. "Abiding in Him consciously, how can the soul but rejoice and be glad? Even when weeping…there is the fountain of gladness springing up in the faith of His power and love to save. And this, His own joy abiding with us, He wants to be *full*."[9]

Moses told God, "If Your Presence does not go with us, do not bring us up from here."[10]

In other words: God, if Your presence is not with me, count me out. I'm not going anywhere without You!

No presence = no joy = no power = no go!

Keep reading, because the supernatural messages kept on coming.

12

NAPS ARE NICE

The reason so many of us are strangers to ourselves is because we don't sit before the Lord. If you want to discover your destiny, you've got to spend time in the presence of God.
—MARK BATTERSON, *SOULPRINT*

June 2015

WITH SUCH INSIGHT and wisdom to ponder, I printed out Josiah's messages and carried them around with me in my SUV, on my walks, you name it. They were folded inside my Bible and journal so I could read them again and again for encouragement. Each time I did, I was amazed and felt my faith soar. Of course, the Word of God remained my plumb line and source of truth. Genuine prophetic words from the Holy Spirit are meant to encourage, illuminate, warn, and draw us closer to Jesus.

Oftentimes I went back and found other nuggets I'd missed or that spoke to me in new ways. Here is an example, just a little instruction from Josiah:

> My hours are nightly my joy with you....Max, breathe on your books the breath of my ruach....Make them banded by hope, maintained by grace.

I knew from my biblical studies that *ruach* is a Hebrew word used to refer to the breath of God, and God's *ruach* is often associated with His creative power. The word first appears in Genesis 1:2: "And the Spirit of God [Ruach Elohim] was hovering over the face of the waters." In Genesis 6:17, *ruach* is translated as "breath of life." It seemed the Spirit of God had moved on Josiah once again to use a word he had no knowledge of. So far in his messages, he used the Hebrew words *dalet*, *sukkah*, and *ruach*.

OK, but what was I supposed to do with this latest nugget?

In response, my intercessory prayer became about reaching that point where *ruach*, the breath of God, could breathe on the pages and I could write what He wanted me to write—words of "hope" and "grace" to a hurting world. I absolutely could not do any writing without the *ruach* of God. What would be the point?

Josiah continued:

> You will be drastically nightly visited by the spirit of artistry over your hands. Joy is the very big house you will be in to make these big nights become your bridge....Let your words bring love to this breaking out of My Spirit. On the branches of My vine for your big God's night brail for your fingers, He makes you feel the words in your fingertips as if you are reading his thoughts...for your God brightens his home in Heaven with your joy. End.

Each line took my breath away. How could any writer not be encouraged by this?

Yes, my desire was for God to work through my fingers, but to be "drastically nightly visited by the spirit of artistry" would be an answer to prayer beyond belief! Most writers, artists, painters, and sculptors would pay a fortune for such a thing. I knew that wasn't how God worked, though. He didn't need money or good works or bribes disguised as prayers. The freedom and divine creativity flowed from intimacy with Him. This was very personal to me, but I knew it was also for everyone. The Holy Spirit wanted to blow on us all with His *ruach*.

I also smiled at the misspelling of braille. I had to look it up myself. We are imperfect vessels even when God works through us, which just makes His grace even more amazing.

Or maybe it was another double meaning.

Alanna later found that the word *brail* describes the ropes used to haul in the edges or corners of sails on a boat.

Needless to say, in nights to come, I sensed an unusual degree of the Lord's *ruach* as I wrote, my "fingertips" moving over the keyboard like "God's night brail…reading his thoughts" even as He tightened my sails for greater speed.

———

July 10, 2016

My initial questions to Tahni had been answered long ago, and we developed a friendship through emails, texts, and phone calls. Her book coauthored with Cheryl Ricker was out, and God was using it to expand her ministry voice. I emailed her an endorsement for her book, but I hadn't received any prophetic messages from Josiah since the previous March, just an encouraging line here and there.

Whoa, was that all about to change!

My wife and I were moved into our new Acadian cottage now, and for the past year, we'd been enjoying our guests and grandchildren. My wonderful new office was at the heart of our home.

It was our war room, my special place of prayer and work. I had learned to play the guitar in college and kept it up over time, but I'd been without one of my own for years. A few months after we moved into the cottage, my kids gave me a new guitar for Christmas. Though I was a little rusty, I added it to my worship times. That was a God story all in itself. As I worshipped there in my office, God's presence was established, and His sweet peace greeted anyone the moment they walked in.

When author and man of God Bruce Van Natta stayed with us, he spent time preparing in my office for ministry at our home church. Later he told me there was an instant anointing he tapped into as he stepped into the room, a deep well he could draw from. He said he benefited from all the hours I'd spent there praying. As Josiah alluded to in his March message, our home—particularly my office—was becoming a bridge for the fulfillment of our assignment.

Another man of God, who moved in the prophetic gifts, said our ministry would reach from my office around the world. This began to unfold quickly before our eyes, with my books spreading into more and more countries.

Because the prayer in this war room was so effective, I was going to the motel on the coast less and less for my sacred times. Instead of praying so much in the evenings, I began studying my Bible and praying in the mornings while Alanna was working and no one else was home. I still did night prayers when prompted, but daybreak became my mainstay for this season. After praying in the mornings so intensely for a couple of hours and then writing for a couple of hours, I was often exhausted and took early afternoon naps. This threw my schedule off, forcing me to do more writing at night, sometimes until 1:00 or 2:00 a.m.

I struggled with guilt over this. I mean, people were out working their jobs while I was curled up for a nap. Granted, my writing schedule was split up so that I put in a full day of work, but it was still a struggle for me to be OK with it.

Thanks to my Josiah journey, I was living with a greater awareness of God's presence, regardless of how I felt. While that sounded elementary, I knew many Christians didn't live in this awareness. And yet it was so vital. It had to be sought and fought for. Being aware of His presence is the key to living a supernatural life and keeping in step with the Holy Spirit's leading. It creates expectancy, which leads to manifestation.

It is critical to schedule extended, uninterrupted, secret moments with God. William Carey, the father of modern Protestant missions, once said, "Prayer—secret, fervent, believing prayer—lies at the root of all personal godliness."[1] Martin Luther declared, "I have so much business, I cannot get on without spending three hours in prayer."[2]

Certainly not everyone can spend three hours a day in the secret place. Some spend much less time, and some spend even more. Sometimes you just have to do what you have to do. In the early 1900s Jonathan and Rosalind Goforth went to China as missionaries. They had eleven children, five of whom died as babies or toddlers. Rosalind was often on her own at home, taking care of the children while her husband was out ministering. It was a tough life. She needed time in God's presence for renewal, but there was nowhere secluded to go. As a faithful mother, she couldn't just leave the children, so she set a chair in the middle of the kitchen and told them in essence, "I am right here. But when you see me with my apron over my head, I will be talking to God. Please do not interrupt me when I am talking with Him unless there is an emergency." Rosalind Goforth created her own spiritual "hot spot," where she connected with Jesus in the middle of her chaos.[3]

No matter the amount of time, it isn't about just fitting Jesus into a busy schedule. It has to be a total lifestyle makeover where He becomes our passion. Knowing Him has to be the main drive of our lives. Even in exceptionally demanding seasons, we have to take advantage of pockets of time and exercise full-out focus.

It is about increasing our availability to Him. As Paul urged in 1 Thessalonians 5:17, it is about praying "without ceasing," living in the awareness of His presence. "I keep my eyes always on the Lord," David wrote. "With him at my right hand, I will not be shaken."[4]

At that point in time, I had my own scheduling issues to juggle. I was under a tight deadline again, collaborating on a new book. As a result, Alanna and I missed church that Sunday as she labored with me on a chapter titled "First Fruits." In it, we wrote about how our firstfruits are important to God, whether they are our money, our time, or our talent. When we offer Him our firstfruits, He gives the rest of our resources maximum effectiveness.

By noon I was depleted and expressed my guilt for needing to crash again.

Alanna, my wielder, said, "It's OK to take a nap, even if you have to write tonight."

This was not the first time she had told me this. Time and again, she said it was OK to nap because it would make me more effective at night. With her blessing, I took a nice long nap that afternoon. I woke up refreshed and went back to writing after dinner and wrote deep into the night.

July 11, 2016

The next morning, a Monday, I received a surprise message from Josiah. It had been over a year since the last prophetic word like this, and I knew right away it was supernatural.

He wrote:

> Naps are nice, aren't they Max? Just naturally naps direct you to just ripe grapes for the picking....Might a nap be nice? Just like motel times...Just because night forces you to join it, look out great napping eyes at times because noting God at first fruit time forces

you to handle a vine with great known picking time.
You have book in the great fort of direction....Just
get our first fruit out, Jesus says, calling you gifted to
pick at the quiet fancy hour of the sweetest grapes he
forges for you.

Holy cow!

After getting this message, I immediately called Tahni to get the scoop. She told me they never took naps or even talked about them. "It'd be a wonderful thing if Josiah ever did take a nap!" she said. Naps were not even on the little boy's brain.

Once again, God was telling me to trust Him and relax. No, I didn't have to live in guilt, because "naps are nice." Take a deep breath...*ruach.*

Even better, "naps" directed me to "ripe grapes for the picking"! There was a "first fruit time," a perfect "picking time," so why was I worried? It wasn't always about sticking to a rigid schedule, but rather giving my full heart to God. I just needed to "get our first fruit out." From my lock of intercession, the Holy Spirit would direct me day and night to the most productive writing/picking times. I often found "the sweetest grapes" during the "quiet fancy hour."

"Wow," I thought. "I was writing about firstfruits just yesterday, and this is what Josiah sends me after a year of basically nothing? God, You're too much!"

Just for fun, I emailed Tahni the "First Fruits" chapter my wife and I had worked on.

As it turns out, Josiah wasn't done yet.

Did a seed dare a grape to form or did a raisin hand
a question as to how dry the life of a waiting farmer
must be if he missed the little window to pick the
grapes and make new wine?...Baffling bold first fruit
farmer...gain a first fruit goblet...being on the ripe
fruit and never on the raisins.

It seemed jumbled, but there was so much depth in it. As with "lining his mine" and "locks installed into his flow," I did an online search, this time for best grape-harvesting times. It was a good thing I was sitting down, because the results blew me away!

Winemakers have discovered there is an optimal "little window to pick the grapes" that produces the best wine. And when is that window of time? Between the middle of the night and the wee hours of the morning, particularly between 3:00 a.m. and sunrise!

"It is part of a worldwide practice that's increasingly the norm for harvesting grapes—in the dead of night," wrote Mirabeau Winery. "It results in better wine, lower energy costs and greater efficiency....There is a small window of opportunity."[5] *Wine Country Table* reported, "Night harvesting has been embraced as the best way to harvest chardonnay wine grapes, with many of the finest wineries in the world practicing the method....By picking when fruit is chilled [at night], the grapes remain clean and fresh. You can taste the difference in the juice even before it's made into wine—it's crisp and rich and dances on the tongue."[6] Another source said, "Picking grapes at night when it is coolest, allows the winemaker to benefit from a natural chilling effect which protects the freshness of the grapes and the purity of the fruit flavour."[7]

Many grape growers still harvest during the day, but the "bold first fruit farmer" harvests at night to get the absolute sweetest grapes for the most delectable wine—and I'm pretty sure those nighttime harvest workers take some daytime naps! I know the feeling. I often find myself writing well into the night or waking up around 4:00 a.m. to head into my office. Not everyone could operate on such a schedule, but you do what you have to do. As "baffling" as it seems, that is what it takes to get the "first fruit goblet."

This was powerful stuff. John 15:4–5 says: "Abide in Me, and I in you. As the branch cannot bear fruit of itself, unless it abides in the vine, neither can you, unless you abide in Me. I am the vine, you are the branches. He who abides in Me, and I in him, bears much fruit; for without Me you can do nothing." Scripture tells us not to be drunk with wine but with the Holy Spirit, and my head was spinning as I let all this settle.

Josiah surely knew his stuff—stuff only the Holy Spirit could reveal to him.

Remember, he was only ten, nonverbal, struggling to tap out each word, unable to surf the internet. One email from him would've been enough. Even a line or two of accurate info would've touched my heart. But he had much more to send my way, every bit of it as insightful and beautiful.

13

IT'S BLURRY

We never grow closer to God when we just live life;
it takes deliberate pursuit and attentiveness.
—FRANCIS CHAN, CRAZY LOVE

September 2016

HAVE YOU EVER had a dream so vivid and specific you thought it was real? I had one that September and knew every single detail because it was unbelievably intense. I was pretty shaken up, and the images wouldn't leave me.

I am always careful about interpreting dreams or calling them prophetic. Though Joseph and Daniel both interpreted dreams in Scripture, they had clear visions from the Lord. There was never any doubt. In my lifetime I've had only a few dreams I considered from God, and this sure seemed like one of those. It contained details and instructions about the future of my writing ministry, and I needed something from the Lord confirming it was from Him.

"What did it all mean?" I wondered. "Was it really You, Lord?"

——

October 12, 2016

I was going through a period of doubt, questioning myself and my calling, and matters only worsened when nearly a month passed without so much as a whisper from God about the dream. Maybe it was all in my head—the dream, my calling, everything. I started treading that ole Max Davis treadmill, running from my inadequacies and insecurities—my mistakes as a young man, my old wounds and my shame, my quirks as an out-of-the-box writer.

Who did I even think I was? Was I actually called by God or just chasing my own tail? Oh, I know it made no sense, and I can imagine people saying to themselves, "Really, even after all these years, published books, and incredible supernatural confirmations? How could he possibly doubt it?" I was seriously struggling, though.

As a writer, I put it all on the line with every book I wrote. Each one is a walk of faith, a marathon that demands incredible mental energy, focus, and another level of reliance on God. The bottom line: writing books is bigger than me and my ability to pull it off. It has to be God. Also, even though He has provided well for me financially, there is no guarantee my next book will even be published. I have to trust Him to continue to provide the contracts.

With all this on my mind, the enemy was relentlessly pounding on me to give up. It was totally a spiritual attack, and lies that seemed ridiculous from a distance sure felt real, sharp, and painful when they were up close.

With clipboard and pen in hand, I drove to the levee trail that runs for miles and miles along the Mississippi River. Over the next three hours, I took one of my prayer walks, crying out: "Is this really You, God? I need to know, because if You don't come through, I'm dead meat! Is writing just some selfish dream I have perpetuated through the years, or is this really an assignment from You? I'm not leaving this place until it's settled!"

In my journalistic way, I went over stages of my life, starting back in high school when God spoke to me that I would write books that would go all over the world. I knew the thought did not come from me, and it seemed audible. At that point, as I stated earlier, I was getting Ds in English and had never even read a book that wasn't filled with pictures. Writing was not something I would have ever thought up for myself, but His voice was as real to me as my little sister's down the hall.

"Was I just an immature, idealistic kid?" I asked God on that levee. "Or was it really You who spoke to me that night? I'm having a hard time remembering! It's blurry."

I actually said that to Him, out loud. "It's blurry."

Fortunately I have kept journals and records since high school that I've looked back to countless times for confirmation. I still have the notes from my senior year when God first spoke to me about being a writer. It has been a difficult road since then, with each step requiring more nerve. My trust in the Lord wavers at times along the way. Hey, I'm not some great man of faith who never has questions or doubts. My assignment of writing still seems too big at times.

Eventually, by the river peace settled into my heart, and I scribbled the following words from the Holy Spirit on my clip-board: "Yes, I was childish and immature, but the calling was real. There was a lot of Max that God had and still has to get out, so He can flow through me more and more."

This was much-needed encouragement from the Lord to take another step forward, but I still wasn't sure about the purpose of the previous month's dream. It was just bugging me.

———

October 14, 2016

Two days later, on a Friday afternoon, I did something I normally didn't do. I sent Tahni a text message explaining I'd had a pro-phetic dream and wondering if she could ask Josiah if he knew anything about it.

"Sure," Tahni replied. "Send me the dream, and I'll read it to him and see what he says."

"No, I would like for you to ask him before I send it," I told her, "to see if he knows anything before hearing the dream."

She said, "Well, I guess how I feel is, I try not to use the 'Do you have a word for [blank]?' questions with Josiah. We can pray and ask God to sovereignly move on Josiah if He has a word... Ha, so I guess it's up to you if you want to wait and see or not."

Tahni's polite refusal to press Josiah for answers didn't surprise me. She was always ethical and authentic with me. She wasn't looking to get anything out of her son or to manipulate me. Her integrity convinced me to agree, and we both decided to wait and see if God would move on Josiah like He had in the past.

I don't know why, but the moment I hung up, I changed my mind and went ahead and forwarded the dream to Tahni.

After praying once more for the Lord to move on Josiah, I turned off my cell phone, picked up my guitar, and began to worship. During one of Bruce Van Natta's visits, he'd told me, "Your guitar is your gate." He meant that when I praised God with my guitar in this space, the gates of the Holy Spirit opened up.

Wow, "dual gates and locks." Those themes from Josiah's message kept coming around.

For a good thirty minutes, maybe longer, I sang, strummed, and shouted praises. Over and over I belted out the words, "You are worthy! You are holy! You are faithful and true! Praise You, Jesus!" I simply loved worshipping Jesus, and joy exploded in my heart as it often did when I offered loud praises to Him. After I set down the guitar, I turned my phone back on. Almost immediately it dinged to indicate a message.

"You must be the most favored man alive," Tahni texted, "because Josiah started typing a word to you. I haven't brought it up to him....God loves you big time. No, I haven't seen your dream piece yet." She continued, "Will eat supper and hopefully get Josiah to comment on that later."

So the message I was getting now was *not* the interpretation of the dream. These were words God had independently given to Josiah for me. The first two sentences were:

> Light Papa lifts up to say to Max. Max, joy is banded
> to your music. It names hosannas to me.

C'mon now.

I had just spent half an hour praising God at the top of my lungs, experiencing this great "joy," and no one knew about that but God and me. Hosanna, another Hebrew word, is defined as "an expression of adoration, praise, or joy." Synonyms include "shouts of praise" and "alleluia."[1] God heard my "hosannas." He was letting me know He saw our times together, which gave me full confidence this message was from Him. Josiah hadn't mentioned my music since January of the previous year when he talked about me banding playlists together for sacred motel times. It was safe to say God valued His people's prayers and praises to Him. Yes, praise was a gate.

The message continued:

> If dreams are big to handle, you are so ideal to hold
> one so managed by you to say reality was blurry....It
> is valuable to hold my gifts as you do.

I knew the boy wasn't talking about the one vivid dream I'd sent to his mom but about my dreams of writing. It was like he'd been eavesdropping on my private prayers!

Think about it. Just two days earlier, I had used some of these exact words in my cries to God along the Mississippi. I'd told Him my "dreams" seemed too "big to handle." I'd asked God specifically if the calling on my life was real and if He really had spoken to me. I needed help because it all seemed "blurry." These were things I said only to God, directly to my Papa. Now, Papa was gently chiding me for trying to "hold one" of my dreams and for keeping it "managed" by my own effort. There was no need for me to question if "reality was blurry." He had spoken to me back in high school and given me an assignment, which He would still bring to harvest in the present and the future. He was my source. Only He could manage it.

The rest of Josiah's message was really personal. It was pro-phetic, accurate, and comforting. To top it off, he ended with:

> He names Max before mom asked. Just for the record,
> Max. Love, Josiah.

That took a second, and then I laughed. The boy had a sense of humor. He was letting the skeptic in me know the Holy Spirit had prompted him to give me this word before his mom even asked him anything. God had heard my cries along the levee trail and my hosannas in my office, and by His Spirit, He shared those private details with Josiah.

All of this was so encouraging, yet the boy still hadn't addressed my specific dream from September. Tahni said she would show it to him after supper, so there was still hope.

Oh, well, I figured, I might just have to wait.

———

Perhaps you're struggling with questions about your own call or assignment. You've waited a long time. You have a dream that makes no sense and doubts that won't go away.

I've been there, and I promise you, your cries are being heard. God is present in the midst of your trials. Psalm 56:8 says He collects your tears in a bottle. Proverbs 3:5–6 says, "Trust in the LORD with all your heart, and lean not on your own under-standing; in all your ways acknowledge Him, and He shall direct your paths."

Seek Him.

Keep your eyes and ears open.

He will give direction at the appropriate time.

14

OLD PERRY

*His [Jacob's] determination to obey, his humble
acknowledgement of God's presence, and his simple, yet heart-
felt prayer, positioned him to do business with God.[1]*
—ROY HICKS JR., *A SMALL BOOK ABOUT GOD*

October 14, 2016

LATER THAT EVENING, Josiah sent a follow-up message. This
was his response to hearing from his mother about my
dream. Sure, I had nudged God's hand a little on wanting this
one, but after a month of waiting, I was desperate for an interpretation. Just because Josiah was given the dream's details didn't
mean he would know what it meant. That would have to come
from God.

I'll share some quick background info before I share what the
boy sent me.

My grandfather was also a Max, and I was named after him
as a sign of respect. To avoid any confusion during my younger
years, my family and relatives called me Perry Max, joining my
first and middle names, rarely just Max. That was all fine until I
started school.

"Perry Max, Perry Max," the kids teased.

It didn't help that I had a buzz cut, which meant I was also
laughed at for being a "bald-headed buzzard." Kids can be harsh.
Who knows what goes on in the mind of a seven-year-old. At any
rate, by third grade I was fed up with it.

I came home one day and gave my parents a matter-of-fact
order: "Never call me Perry again! Just call me Max." Max
sounded tough.

From then on, Perry was dropped and I was known simply as Max—unless I got into trouble. Then Perry Max was resurrected. When the two names were paired together, it usually meant I'd gotten into some sort of mischief or done something childish and silly—which was a lot of the time. In my ultra-legalistic, religious background, I couldn't count how many times I heard, "God's going to punish you, Perry Max!"

All this only reinforced what I already knew at that time about God and myself—that He was mad and disappointed in me. I was a no-good sinner.

Somehow over the years, Perry got subconsciously linked to my negative emotions and insecurities. This was highlighted in 2009 while I was going through a particularly trying time, battling self-doubt. One night a dark figure appeared at my bedside and started poking me in the middle of my forehead with its long, bony finger, taunting, "Perry, Perry, Perry."

The experience shook me up, and I shared it with Chris, a man God used regularly to speak into my life. Though Chris is one of my best friends, he'd never even heard my first name, and he asked me who Perry was. After I explained the whole thing to him, he fixed me in his gaze and said, "God wants to heal you of 'old Perry.' He wants you to embrace Perry Max."

A great healing began to take place in my life that day. Over time I embraced my full identity and even considered putting Perry Max on future books. Regardless I was still a work in progress and had lingering insecurities God was working on.

My dream from the previous month stirred many of those old questions. In the dream, I was walking through a pasture of cows when I noticed something wasn't right. There were three moons in the sky. It was surreal, and I had the distinct sense that time was short on earth. Suddenly some of the cows sprouted wings and flew off into the distance, and then other cows with no wings got sucked up straight into the sky and disappeared. Was this the rapture? Why wasn't I taken up? Where were my wings? I cried out to God, "I don't know what else to do! I trusted the gospel!"

As I walked along, it felt as if I was trudging through deep mud; then my feet started morphing into the ground. I could not move. As I struggled to free myself, a tarp-like sheet dropped over me, holding me down. I was completely trapped. Light shone through the tarp, and I could make out shadows of men preparing to take me somewhere I didn't want to go. I also noticed the tarp was stamped with logos and people's names in the publishing business. I thrashed to no avail, and then...I woke up.

It was all so serious and disturbing. What did it mean?

Now I had something from Josiah, and I held my breath as I read his response:

> If cows are bold...are those cows made to join you... investing in limiting fluttering faith in riches you might have today and might leave tomorrow? Cows don't have wings...If you largely pant for the life of the earth, you will paper it with more logos.

In Scripture, cows are often used in illustrations. For example, the seven fat cows and seven skinny cows of Pharaoh's dream referred to seven years of abundance followed by seven of hunger.[2] I realized this dream had to do with my writing assignment from the Lord, finances, and timing. Even those "cows" that were "bold" and sprouting wings were not necessarily ones "made to join" me. The purpose of my books wasn't to have "fluttering faith in riches." If I started to "pant for the life of the earth" and its temporary rewards, I would only "paper it with more logos." It wasn't my job to promote other people or publishers, but God alone!

Josiah had more to say:

> Long for material pleasant to light up larger life as bold as bold is planning for you...making it worth it to you. Love the name of life....Just name one more

> limit old Perry is molding to…questions are faster
> when art is weighed by God not reasonable golden
> people you admire.

Whoa, now. This was even more amazing—and a little exposing.

In nearly two years and twenty printed pages, Josiah had always referred to me as Max. Very few people outside my family knew my first name, and it wasn't on any public materials I was aware of. I had never shared this information with Tahni or Josiah. This time, however, when driving home his point, Josiah called me "old Perry." It wasn't the jeering playground name or the dark figure's taunt but the term Chris used when he talked to me about being healed. Instead of labeling me, the Holy Spirit was confirming it was time to put the past to rest.

The meaning here was complex and personal. In essence, Josiah was saying the dream was about how I put limits on myself and allowed others to do the same. He was challenging me to "love the name of life" I'd been given at birth and let go of hurts and fears I'd been "molding to."

As a writer, I had constant decisions to make about contracts, deadlines, coauthors, publishers. I often let "reasonable golden people" I admired bend me into their way of thinking. My reasoning was they were more experienced and knowledgeable than me. I should yield to them. I kind of knew better but let myself be influenced anyway. It's hard to stand up to those you hold in such high esteem. This didn't mean I shouldn't get their good counsel and wise advice, but God is my final authority, and His scales alone determine the worth of my words.

Once again, Josiah nailed it. My "questions" were dealt with "faster when" my "art" was "weighed by God." If I got wrapped up in prestige or ego or pleasing others, I just got mired even deeper in self-doubt. It was time to embrace who I was—Perry Max Davis, created by God to be obedient and courageous, unique and like no other! I was not to settle for less but "long for material pleasant to light up larger life as bold as bold is planning for you...making it worth it to you."

I'm not the only one with negative thoughts. Maybe the failures, ridicules, and accusations of your past keep popping into your head. They're hard and loud as nails—"pop pop pop."

Listen to me, please. I can tell you this as a fact.

You have a "papa papa papa" who cares for you more than you can fathom.

God, your heavenly Papa, wants you to break free from those things so you can see Him and not your past or your old self. Maybe you haven't experienced some dark figure hovering over you, but self-disdain can be just as treacherous. Focusing on your flaws and weaknesses only draws your attention away from the Lord. Even focusing on other good "reasonable golden people" can cause you to miss what God is trying to do in and through you.

You are His child, His precious child. Don't let what earthly fathers, mothers, and others have done, good or bad, block your view of the one Papa who truly sees you, knows you, and loves with the purest of all loves.

God *is* love. From His love comes *grace*.

His grace is sufficient for all His children, including *you*.

Ask for God's healing touch to break those strongholds. Ask for forgiveness for your sins, and lay aside the weights and sins that hold you down.

When things from my past creep into my head, I am learning to speak truths and promises from the Word of God. Hebrews 2:18 tells us since Jesus Himself has gone through suffering and testing, He is able to help us when we are being tested. He was flesh and blood, and He sympathizes with our weaknesses.[3] He remembers we are but dust.[4] This doesn't change the fact that you are nothing short of a miracle in your Father's eyes. "But now thus says the LORD," in Isaiah 41:3, "he who created you, O Jacob, he who formed you, O Israel: 'Fear not, for I have redeemed you; I have called you by name, you are mine'" (ESV).

You are no accident.

You are fearfully and wonderfully made, fashioned in His image.

Do you hear that? The Good Shepherd cares for His sheep, and He will go after you no matter how far you've strayed. He is on His way, even if it means leaving the rest of the flock to find you, tend to your wounds, and carry you back on His shoulders.[5]

15

GOOD THINGS OR GOD THINGS

*I have begun to see that worship and intercession are
far more the business of aligning myself with God's
purposes than asking Him to align with mine.*
—GORDON MACDONALD, *ORDERING YOUR PRIVATE WORLD*

August 10, 2018

AFTER HEARING FROM Josiah on October 14, 2016, nearly two years went by with nothing from him—nada, zip, not a peep. Tahni and I continued our friendship via phone. Meanwhile, her son was growing up.

At the time of my first encounter with Josiah Cullen, in early 2015, he was only nine and about four feet tall. Now he was almost thirteen and shooting up like a weed. His body was going through all the stages of adolescence, which brought new challenges yet some wonderful breakthroughs too. For example, Josiah picked up a paintbrush for the first time and started turning out incredibly unique masterpieces. People could view some of his artwork on his *Josiah's Fire* Facebook page, and when I saw one of his paintings, I immediately thought he should have his own gallery in New York or LA!

Still non-speaking, Josiah got frustrated wanting to communicate all that was locked up in his head. The struggle amplified his teen tensions, and he began hitting himself, banging on things, yelling loudly, and covering himself in layers of blankets and clothing. Often he retreated for days into his own private world of autism. Josiah experienced both good days and bad. On the good ones, as in this 2018 picture with his mom, the Cullen family could go on fun outings together, but on the difficult ones, Josiah was unable to even go out in public.

Because of these latest challenges and the fact that I hadn't heard from him in nearly two years, I figured the prophetic messages were over.

Boy, was I wrong!

That Friday in August, I met my friend Chris for lunch again. I had so much to discuss with him.

Back in 2015, not knowing what to do with my Josiah encounters, I hadn't shown the messages to anyone but a few family members and friends. Nevertheless, questions weighed on my mind. Why did God give me this gift? Obviously it was to encourage and direct me, and I was grateful. But was it just for me? Should I be sharing it with others? After all, I was a writer. Stories were what I did, and this was a humdinger!

I began praying about it, then expressed my dilemma to a well-respected pastor of a large conservative Baptist church.

"Max," he told me, "God gave you this experience for a reason. He wants to encourage your soul, but understand, the clearer the word, the harder the assignment. You will go through some dark moments, but live in hope and rest. The dark will be very dark yet will pass. Do not dread. It will be a war."

OK, as sobering as that was, I knew it was true. God had used Josiah over the past two years to encourage me to stay the course no matter how rocky the road got.

"Still," I wondered, "what about writing down these encounters for others?"

One day, while I was shopping, of all things, the Holy Spirit dropped into my spirit, "Just write up the story in a basic way and give it out to the individuals I lead you to. Watch what I do. Then you will have your answer."

So that's what I did.

And the responses were over the top! I'm talking lives altered, people brought out of deep depression, fires for Jesus ignited and rekindled, even a radical atheist impacted.

Ron DiCianni, an internationally renowned artist, wrote to me after reading my messages from Josiah, "I think you are privileged that God chose a young, innocent boy to speak to you. He doesn't do it that way with everyone. It's what you do with it now that is important....Hope it turns into more for God."

After Ron's email and other responses, I knew it was my responsibility to be a good steward of this incredible gift and get it into as many hands as possible. Turning it into "more for God" was my whole goal. As I began writing about it, the spiritual warfare intensified. That was no surprise. It seemed everything but the kitchen sink was thrown at me, trying to get me to give up and leave the book undone. The agitations pulling at me were never-ending—good things, distractions, confusion, interruptions, fear of what others would think, fear of the "doctrine police," you name it.

Alanna and I were at a crowded party one evening when Maria, a woman who knew nothing about my encounters with Josiah, pulled the two of us aside. Tears spilled down her cheeks, and she pleaded with us in her thick Hispanic accent, "There's a book you have to write! You must understand, things are going to happen to try to prevent you from writing it. Don't give up! It's going to show people to the Lord. People are dying without knowing Jesus!" She took both my hands in hers and squeezed tightly. "You'll know what to write. It's going to bring people to know Him. Don't let anything stop it!" Her grip tightened, her eyes glistening as she shook me. "You must write this book. You must!"

My wife and I shared understanding glances because we knew exactly what Maria was talking about. Only Alanna knew what I'd been wrestling with, warring with, what a battle this project had been, unlike anything else I'd ever written.

Despite Maria's words to me, it wasn't long before I was on the verge again of throwing in the towel. The obstacles were too many. They were taking a toll on me and my family. That's when I had a night vision more real than any dream, with every color and image and pixel distinct, as if I were watching it on HDTV.

In the vision, I was talking on my phone to a young atheist. "Have I got a story for you," I told him. "It proves God is real and sees us when we call out to Him. Do you want to hear it?"

"Yes," he replied, his voice catching. "Please, tell me."

As soon as I tried, my words came out slurred and unintelligible. "Please," he urged again. "Tell me!"

I gave it another shot, but with no success, and the more I wrestled with my tongue, the more garbled my speech became. I decided to read the story to him straight from the pages in my hand. When I did, the typed words became scrambled, making them impossible to read!

"Please, *tell* me!" the young man begged for a third time.

No matter how hard I tried, though, I couldn't do it. Nothing. Not a word. He needed hope, and I was useless.

Then it hit me. Some evil force was jumbling everything, trying to prevent the story from being shared. I yelled at the top of my lungs, "It's supernatural!"

When I did, a ten-foot-tall demon appeared just over my shoulder, its skin red and black and burnt to a crisp. It wore a nasty scowl, its focus on my pages in hand. As soon as our eyes locked, it let out the most ferocious, terrifying roar, and that gale-force wind shook my entire body. I bolted upright in my bed, wide awake and sweating.

The whole episode reminded me of Paul's night vision in the Book of Acts, when he saw a Macedonian man calling him to come and preach the gospel. It was so real to him that he "at once" adjusted his course to Macedonia.[1] It became crystal clear that God was telling me, "This story is critical, Max. Lives are going to be impacted—atheists, skeptics, young, old, the wounded and hurting. Believers are going to be encouraged in their faith and drawn into more intimate relationships with Jesus. But beware, all hell is going to try and stop it. Never mind that; just get the story out!"

I knew then that I could not give up.

I usually write more than one book at a time. At that point in 2018 I had three other projects under contract while trying to write the Josiah book too—four total! They were all good stories with strong messages, and I wondered how to proceed.

That Friday over lunch, Chris and I discussed the fact that both of us were getting older and had to be more responsible with the gifts God had for us. I told him that some of my potential writing projects were not in my actual gifting flow, often sucking the inspiration and creativity from me. God had given me an assignment and a lane to move in, and I needed to be accountable to that. Even good things, even other projects offered to me, were knocking me out of alignment and out of my lane assignment.

"Max, if it's not life-giving," Chris said, "you can't do it, regardless of the money or the big name. There is a well-intended conspiracy to keep you distracted from fulfilling your assignment. This is dangerous in your life, Max. Other people applying pressure, pulling on you... We are responsible to steward the time left in our lives focusing on our true gifts."

I knew I wasn't the only one who got bogged down doing good things when called to do God things. I couldn't be irresponsible with my necessary obligations, of course, but moving toward God's goals meant saying no to things that could distract or derail me, no matter how good they seemed.

After lunch with Chris, I went back to my home office. I had two index cards on my desk for inspiration and focus. I'd written on one, and Alanna had written on the other. The first said, "STAY IN YOUR LANE. DO WHAT YOU ARE GIFTED TO DO." The second had the words "stay in your lane" underlined in red. Countless times, Alanna, my wielder, had said those words to me.

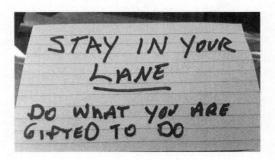

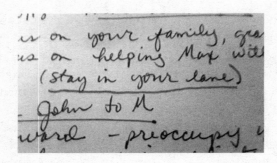

If all this wasn't confirmation enough, I received a message from Josiah the next day. Really? After nearly two years?

To say I was surprised would be a huge understatement.

16

PICTURED LANES LIT UP FOR YOU

[God] gives us Himself through the Person of the Holy Spirit so the assignment can be accomplished. That understanding frees us to accept all that the Father calls us to do with joy and confidence.
—CHARLES F. STANLEY, *COURAGEOUS FAITH*

August 11, 2018

THAT SATURDAY MORNING, I was in full-blown panic mode. One of my book projects was stressing me out, and my wife and I were discussing it in my office. She reminded me about my previous day's lunch with Chris and about focusing on my gifts and staying in my lane assignment.

"This is distracting and derailing you," she said. "It's keeping you from the flow of the Holy Spirit and from writing what you should be writing."

I knew Alanna was right. I had a difficult time saying no. I liked people and wanted to help them. I also liked the income and sense of security my writing contracts brought. The problem was I often wound up with too much on my plate.

Josiah had mentioned this in a snippet from one of his earlier messages to me:

> Max Davis bite off loud, big, poor joy if he is not mea-suring up to his load on his plate?

Yep, that was me, "not measuring up," with too big of a "load."

My wife and I continued our conversation there in my office, going over finances, gifting, time management, and how I needed to stay in my lane while good and bad forces tried to drag me back and forth. It was a critical moment, and we were still talking when my cell phone dinged.

It was Tahni Cullen, and she simply wrote, "Incoming."

My jaw dropped. Out of the blue, after all this time, I realized I was about to receive a totally unsolicited, unexpected, sovereign message from the Lord.

The first part of it read:

> Max, nothing is more important this hour, this moment, this day in life, than moving in the pictured lanes lit up for only you. Boldly might you give it old holy longing to stay in the lanes directly given to you? Love, Papa.

You had to be kidding me! The timing was as precise as a nuclear clock, the words ticking off each point so clearly. Chris and I had discussed lanes and assignments. The index cards on my desk spoke of them too. Alanna was in my office reminding me of them even at that moment.

And Josiah used those exact same words!

What more did I need? My loving "Papa" was warning me as loudly as He could that it was "important this hour, this moment, this day" to do as He had assigned. God wasn't asking me to run in the dark. He had "pictured lanes lit up" for me! The only way to "stay in the lanes" I was given was to limit my choices to projects that matched up with my gift set.

I hadn't shared any of my recent turmoil with Tahni. I still hadn't met Josiah in person, with him being over twelve hundred miles away, but the Holy Spirit was making sure that fearful, stubborn Max Davis in Louisiana got the message loud and clear.

Next, Josiah wrote:

> Might nights be a nice time for getting boundaries, to get your nights milled is to make very large big intercession for the mornings to be loudly miraculous....
> Jabberers get no place in your life if My boundaries

are nice and clear. Father brings you more maps of
your loud territory if you make Him your gates in his
building of your giftings.

Boy, it wasn't hard to see how these words applied. Alanna
and I often discussed how not having good, healthy "boundaries"
caused us to drift from our lanes and even collide with other
runners. The Holy Spirit was my lane. When I stayed in alignment with Him, I could write the words He would have me write
to touch the hearts He would have me touch.

Keeping "boundaries" that were "nice and clear" also meant
keeping the "jabberers" at bay. These were the people who
wanted a piece of me—my time, energy, emotion, or resources.
They pulled me out of the Spirit's flow and kept me from com-
pleting my God-given assignment. I couldn't allow them to steal
away precious moments God would have me spend with Him
and spend doing His work. "Above all else," Proverbs 4:23 says,
"guard your heart, for everything you do flows from it" (NIV). The
hardest part was discerning between the "jabberers" and those
who really needed my prayers, attention, and encouragement.

I thought about what "milled" means. When it comes to rice
and other grains, milling gets rid of the husks, excess particles,
and other waste. Josiah was saying at night I needed to sift and
let go of the excess so I could enter into "big intercession." The
best place to get clarity was in God's presence. If I did this, the
start of each day could be "loudly miraculous" and He could
bring me "more maps," broadening my "territory" while guiding
me every step of the way.

The message ended with:

> God notes your many pulls....Look on your gifting
> knowing that more is not more. Look out to limit
> life's maps to your holy points of lighting up the gifts
> in you. Love, Josiah.

Wow, was God gracious!

Emotion caught in my throat as I shared the words with my wife. It was too much. My heavenly Father knew the "many pulls" on my time and resources. He didn't shame me or punish me. He gently, but firmly, reminded me to get back in my lane. I couldn't get distracted by "more" contracts, "more" money, "more" validation. If I did, I would end up all over "life's maps." There was no choice but to obey, "limit" myself to His call, and remind myself I would be held accountable for my time and gifts.

And what about you?

When God speaks, His words often ripple out beyond their initial impact point, so what is He saying to you? Of course, I want you to like me; that's in my nature. But this book is in your hands for a reason, and I have to be direct.

As born-again believers, our lives in Christ are likened to running a race, not just a sprint but an endurance race. Paul urges us to run that race to win! "Do you not know that those who run in a race all run, but one receives the prize? Run in such a way that you may obtain it."[1] How do we run to win? "Let us strip off every weight that slows us down, especially the sin that so easily trips us up. And let us run with endurance the race God has set before us. We do this by keeping our eyes on Jesus, the champion who initiates and perfects our faith."[2]

Paul was drawing from his knowledge of the Olympic Games in Greece. Just as in modern track meets, each runner had an assigned lane. If runners veered outside their lanes, they were disqualified. One thing that keeps you in your lane is keeping your eyes fixed on Jesus. When you do this, your eyes are not fixed on a dead, historical figure, but on a person who is alive! If your focus shifts from Him to others in their lanes, you drift, and that's not good.

Back then, just like today, the starting points were sometimes staggered, meaning the person in the center lane started the race farther back from the runners in the outside lanes. At the beginning, it appeared uneven and unequal.

It even seemed *unfair*.

Have you ever used that word? Perhaps you have thought it or whispered it. Perhaps you've yelled it at the top of your lungs.

I'm here to tell you, we are all at different stages in the race, and comparison will only discourage and frustrate you. Keep focused on the ultimate prize, which is Jesus. Stay in *your* lane, and look ahead to what He has for only *you*.

There *is* a reward, I promise.

Yep, we'll get to that by the end of this book.

———

September 2018

A few weeks after Josiah's email, I spent several days in Lynchburg, Virginia, collaborating on another writing project. It was definitely in my lane. We finished our work on Friday evening, but my flight didn't leave until Saturday afternoon.

With some free time that Saturday morning, I connected for breakfast with a friend named Leonard, who lived in Lynchburg. Like my friend Chris, Leonard moves in the prophetic realm and had spoken into my life before.

As we talked, I looked up and said, "Leonard, I believe you have a word for me."

I was so hungry for more of God I couldn't help prodding it along now and then. This time, though, my friend seemed rattled and didn't really give me much. Still, over the next hour as I shared some of the recent things I'd been learning, I sensed he was wrestling with something. As I told him about Josiah's latest message, Leonard stopped me.

"Wait," he said. "I have something to tell you."

"OK."

"Earlier, when you asked me if I had a word for you, the Holy Spirit said to me in that moment, 'Tell him to stay in his lane.' I argued with myself, thinking it was stupid and wouldn't make any sense if I said that to you."

It was safe to say, God wanted to make sure I remembered His instructions.

As I was driving to the airport, Leonard sent me a text that said, "Max, I enjoyed our time together so much! I've been contemplating all that we said. I actually learned a valuable lesson from that word. Say what the Holy Spirit says when He says it."

Wow. That was a valuable lesson for me too. It is so easy to let doubts or skepticism get in the way of what God wants to say through us. In addition to having our eyes focused on Jesus, we have to strip off the weights and sins that hinder us and slow us down.

Do you know which sins are hindering you?

Sure you do. Most of us do.

Weights are often harder to identify because they aren't necessarily sins. They can even be good things, just not the particular things we are supposed to be doing. Running in someone else's lane or running in two lanes at once while carrying someone else's calling will make you lose focus and feel weighed down. That's no way to run an effective, victorious race.

Not long ago tears streamed down my face as I listened to an incredible interview with a missionary couple who literally left everything and moved to a remote part of Africa. Story after story was told of how God miraculously used them. When the interview was over, I told God, "I want to do that! I want to be a missionary." Totally unexpected, the Spirit of God rose up in me and said, "Never say that again! Do what I told you to do. Write books. You are a missionary, and your books will go where you can never go and reach people that others can't."

Since then the issue has been settled for me, and I have a box of letters from people all over the world whose lives have been touched through my writing—prisoners, students, people overseas, homeless people, atheists, and more.

Stay in your lane, Max. Stay in your lane.

In order to win the prize, each of us is accountable to run the race set before *us* and to stay in *our* lane. Ephesians 5:17 says, "Therefore do not be unwise, but understand what the will of the Lord is." God has given each of us a specific assignment that is His will for us. Discovering your assignment is serious. If you don't discover, value, and use your gifts, it's so easy to fall short of all God has for you. Romans 12:6 says, "Having then gifts differing according to the grace that is given to us, let us use them."

Learn to say no, and stay focused on your gifting. If you're not sure what that gifting is, ask the Lord to make it known to you. He's not playing guessing games. He's not just waiting for you to lose focus and be disqualified. No; He has "pictured lanes lit up for only you."

He wants you to run and feel His glory.

He wants you to win!

17

FACE-TO-FACE

Child, to say the very thing you really mean, the whole
of it, nothing more or less or other than what you
really mean; that's the whole art and joy of words.
—C. S. Lewis, *Till We Have Faces*

October 26, 2018

I was leaving today, and excitement pumped through my veins. I hadn't slept a wink. Tomorrow I would meet Josiah Cullen in person. Almost four years had passed since my first message from him. Since then I'd collected a journal full of printed pages, hand-scrawled notes, and Scripture references. It was time for a face-to-face meeting with the Cullen family.

I arrived at the airport several hours early, my flight from Baton Rouge scheduled to get me to Minneapolis–St. Paul that evening. With all that spare time at the airport, I browsed the gift shops and paced the carpet at the boarding gate. You would have thought I was going to meet POTUS or Billy Graham or some bigwig in the publishing biz, certainly not a thirteen-year-old autistic boy!

After landing at my destination a few hours later, I grabbed a rental car and checked into a hotel. Tahni had warned me on the phone earlier that Josiah was experiencing a rough week, and I wondered how things would go the next day.

"No expectations," I told myself. "Trust God to do what He wants to do."

October 27, 2018

I was up at 6:30 a.m., my stomach churning with butterflies and my mind racing.

How would Josiah react to me? Would he be glad to see me?

I left the hotel early and walked around downtown St. Paul, taking in the beautiful fall trees, praying and trying to let my spirit settle. Then I made my way to Josiah's rural suburb about forty-five minutes away. With an hour till our meeting, I cruised around and found a park with a nature trail winding through the woods where I could walk and pray some more.

Along the trail, I had a God moment. As I stood among the trees, stillness washed over me and replaced my anxiousness with peace. It was as if Jesus were standing right beside me, similar to when I sat in the freedom of Jesus in the woods on our property. Scripture declared He was always present, He was in us, and I sensed His nearness in those few precious minutes.

OK. Now I actually felt ready to meet Joe, Tahni, and Josiah.

Little did I know, what I was about to encounter would make the miracle of Josiah's messages to me even more profound.

Emerging from the woods, I locked in the Cullens' address on my phone's GPS. It was seven minutes away. As I weaved through the unassuming neighborhood, I wondered how many people had passed their house over the years and never known that the autistic boy inside regularly heard from God, that the Creator of the universe sovereignly spoke to him. Similarly, how many of us passed right by the profound things of God every day? If we would only put down our phones or lists of things to do and seek Him, we would find Him. "That they should seek the Lord," declares Acts 17:27, "in the hope that they might grope for Him and find Him, though He is not far from each one of us."

I knocked on the front door, and it opened seconds later. Joe and Tahni seemed genuinely excited to meet me. As I stepped into the foyer, I was instantly put at ease by their warm and welcoming air. Joe was tall, six feet two or six feet three, with an easy manner, kind eyes, and a friendly smile. Tahni had a similarly pleasant demeanor, but her pretty blue eyes revealed a maturity beyond her years. Clearly life had thrown both of them a curveball. They were past being impressed by people and things. Still, a peace enveloped both of them.

This was our first face-to-face meeting, and it took a few moments for all of us to adjust. They led me to the dining room, where we sat and visited and waited for pizza to be delivered.

Where was Josiah? I had expected him to meet me with open arms, but he was nowhere to be found. Tahni had warned me, hadn't she? Her son was having a bad stretch, and she didn't want me to arrive with unrealistic expectations. My response had been, "No problem. I'm cool. I just want to tell the boy who changed my life that I love him."

I had no clue.

About then, a loud screech, wail, or whatever you wanted to call it echoed down the hallway from one of the bedrooms. Josiah's parents continued talking to me as if nothing had happened. More groans came from down the hall. I went with it, figuring they knew what they were doing. They dealt with this every day.

After about thirty minutes and a whole lot of moaning, I seriously wondered if I had come all this way for nothing. Even if Josiah was struggling, couldn't they let him out to see me?

"Does Josiah have to stay in his room?" I finally asked.

"Oh, no," Tahni replied, calm and reassuring. "Josiah can come out anytime he wants."

"Oh." I was a little puzzled. "Did he know I was coming?"

"Yes, we told him. But like I said, he's having a bad day."

"Is he nervous or overly excited because I'm here? Maybe it's got him stirred up."

"No." Tahni exchanged a brave glance with her husband.

"Josiah would be like this whether you were here or not. It has nothing to do with you. He's just had a bad week."

More moans came from the bedroom. I had nothing helpful to say.

The pizza came, and the three of us ate and talked around the table. We learned more about one another. I shared some of my own heartaches God had brought me through—how over the years, I had struggled to communicate with my own son, who was deaf, and how God had showed up time and time again in our lives. Joe, Tahni, and I all understood the pain and frustration of watching someone we loved suffer. This gave us a great connection.

Over an hour passed—still no Josiah.

He didn't even come out to eat his pizza.

As our conversation wound down, my throat tightened. I couldn't leave here like this—not after all these years, not after everything God had done. Please, I didn't want to be left with this sour taste of disappointment. What could I do? Clearly, Joe and Tahni were incredibly patient with Josiah. They loved their son more than themselves and were fully committed to him. They knew they couldn't force these things with Josiah. They just had to go with the flow and let things unfold in their own time.

It was a good lesson for everyone, one I would remember. At that moment, though, I wasn't in the mood for lessons. I had tossed and turned and paced and prayed and flown all this way for a reason. As awkward as it was, I finally asked, "Can we go see him?"

"Sure," Tahni said. "Let's go."

Relief.

Joe and Tahni led me down the hall to Josiah's bedroom, a normal teenage boy's room with bunk beds. Josiah was an only child, but the dual beds made me wonder if they had considered having another at some point before their son was diagnosed as autistic. Josiah was sitting on the bottom bunk beneath a pile of blankets, engrossed in a game or something he had loaded on his tablet. His face was sunk back in the shadows, blue eyes dark behind his glasses.

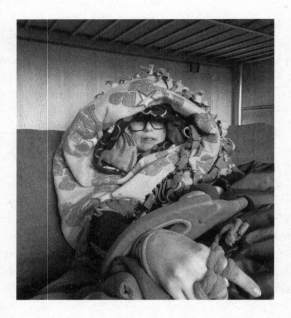

Holding back my emotion, I couldn't believe I was actually face-to-face with Josiah, the boy God had used to wreck my life in a profoundly wonderful way. Here he was, hiding under a blanket in a rural Minnesota town. It was surreal.

"Hey, Josiah," Tahni said. "Max is here to talk to you. You want to say hi?"

No response. The boy's eyes stayed fixed on his tablet screen.

My anxieties faded, and I felt surprisingly at ease. "I love you, Josiah," I said. "Thank you for letting God use you to speak to me. You've changed my life."

For a microsecond he peeked at me from under the blanket.

I longed to hug him but didn't dare set him off or anything.

Already his attention was back on the tablet, and I wondered if I would get any more response out of him.

Then he let out a loud moan.

And another.

Tahni scooted to one side of him, and Joe sat on the other. I took my place in the beanbag chair across the room. We just made ourselves comfortable and talked among ourselves as if everything were normal.

Again, Joe and Tahni's commitment and unconditional love for their son was humbling. I thought of another project I was working on, a book on godly manhood, in which I'd discovered that the number one request for young boys across the country was they just wanted their dads to show up. It was clear to me Joe was an incredible father, and one of the reasons was because he was present. He showed up for both Tahni and Josiah.

"Oh, before I forget," I said, "I have a few gifts for you, Josiah."

I had shopped carefully at the Mall of Louisiana, laboring to find the perfect stuff for him. I had called Tahni for his sizes and likes. Together his parents and I now set everything out—a purple and gold Louisiana State University Tigers cap, a matching LSU jacket, and a shirt with a tiger's eye on it.

I got zero response.

After the adults visited a while longer, Tahni retrieved a laminated cardboard keyboard. This, she explained, was more convenient for Josiah when communicating with people. She would hold it up, and he would touch one fingertip to one letter at a time.

"Would you like to tell Max something?" she asked her son.

Josiah stuck out a single, shaky finger, reaching for the keyboard. I watched him independently tap the letter *A*. Tahni in no way guided him. Once his selection was made, she confirmed it aloud, and I typed it into my phone. He groaned, pulling back into his blanket cave.

"Come on, Josiah. You can do it," Tahni urged. She waited for his next move.

With more shaking and moaning, he continued. I observed the entire process, and it took him every bit of five minutes to type one sentence:

Able to really rope joy using mother's voice. I love you.

My heart leaped inside me. Those few words were worth the whole trip. Though outwardly Josiah seemed detached, he was hearing and receiving everything. I thought back to that very first message in January 2015 when he used the Hebrew letter *dalet* to describe his mother. She was truly the doorway for the words God spoke through him.

The four of us continued to visit. At some point Josiah decided he would labor for a few more minutes and plunk out another sentence:

Max totally nice…in LSU style. Yes.

What really struck me was the massive amount of time and effort that went into these two short sentences. And to think I'd received over twenty pages of single-spaced messages! It was incredible. Watching the process in person, I knew I would value each page more than ever. Tahni explained that on Josiah's good days, he could type much quicker on his tablet, though it was still a significant struggle.

Eventually we persuaded Josiah to stand, and I was able to give him a hug.

One of my high points was getting to pray for Joe, Tahni, and Josiah. It was short, the prayer rolling off my tongue, yet I felt a warm peace and love for these people. Through this unusual and supernatural connection with their son, we had become family. Our time eventually wound down, and we said our goodbyes. The meeting was not at all what I envisioned, but it was perfect. It was perfect because I saw the raw, sober truth up close and personal. It wasn't pretty and sweet but difficult and unsettling.

Josiah struggled. Joe and Tahni struggled.

There was pain, much pain. There were frustrations, questions, fatigue.

It was a tough life. Yet through the cracks and brokenness, light flickered. Jesus was fully present, and His light glowed. There was love and tenderness, warmth and hope. There was joy—not the joy that the world gave but the joy that came from the Holy Spirit.

When the apostle Peter was about to be put to death for his faith, he said, "For we did not follow cunningly devised fables when we made known to you the power and coming of our Lord Jesus Christ, but were eyewitnesses of His majesty."[1] The same was true for Josiah and Tahni. They hadn't birthed some cunningly devised plan to manipulate me. I was now an eyewitness, and I knew that idea was ridiculous. No; Josiah's messages were typed spontaneously through pain and endurance, patience and stress, frustration and sleeplessness—and through love, pure love, his parents laying down their time as the Holy Spirit moved through their son in uncommon, unexplainable ways to give hope to this writer way down in Louisiana.

———

I was in the rental car about an hour later when I got a text from Tahni saying, "Great seeing you today! I asked Josiah if he enjoyed seeing you. This is what he typed."

I whipped the car over and read:

Max is giving him naming to give kisses to me, to say
I'm like a very important person to him....Hugs, Max.
I light up to see you. Mailing my huge gift would have
been just fine, but you got in a plane and wittily flew
in to make me gain a gift in mounted appreciation for
my faithfulness to baffle you with God's ready words
in life. Loudly, might I know you are banded to me?
Love, Josiah.

My face wet with tears, I texted my thanks to Tahni for letting
me visit and for passing this on to me. Josiah's words were the
final assurance I needed that this trip had achieved its purpose.
He and I had connected on a deep level through the Holy Spirit.

Later I sent the dear boy his own follow-up message.

"Josiah," I wrote, "thank you for letting me come visit you. You
are a fine young man and I love you so much. And yes, we are
banded together for life. Love, Perry Max."

18

WHEN GOD DOESN'T MAKE SENSE

*If you have a God great and transcendent enough to be mad at
because he hasn't stopped evil and suffering in the world, then
you have (at the same moment) a God great and transcendent
enough to have good reasons for allowing it to continue
that you can't know. Indeed, you can't have it both ways.*

—TIMOTHY KELLER, *THE REASON FOR GOD*

December 2018

BACK HOME, I continued to process my meeting with the Cullens over the next six or seven weeks. Honestly there was a lot I just didn't understand. I had seen Josiah up close and realized how severe his condition was. I questioned how God could speak through this boy in such profound ways and yet allow him to remain autistic. You would think if an all-powerful, all-knowing God spoke through someone like that, He would heal him too, not sit back and let the boy and his parents suffer. It didn't make sense, not to my natural mind.

This led me to ponder whether my encounters were the real thing. Was the God of the universe actually speaking through Josiah's messages? Or was it possible they were just warm and fuzzy stories involving a ton of wild and crazy coincidences?

My journalistic nature kicked back in, and I scoured the messages several more times with a fine-toothed comb, trying to find any places where I might have missed something or to see if maybe there was a catch I had overlooked. Even if Tahni herself had somehow influenced Josiah, there was no way she could have known even 5 percent of the stuff in the messages—not to mention I'd been in the Cullen home and watched with my own eyes as Josiah typed out sentences to me in his odd syntax.

The bottom line: the messages were too specific and too accurate, and Josiah had not been off with one thing in nearly three and a half years, not a single one. What if Josiah said I was a "novel writer" and I wasn't? What if I didn't like "banding" my "music" for "sacred times at motels"? Or if I didn't have a passion to collect "miracle stories" and journalistically "name them as miracles"? What if I wasn't a "barn man" with "animals" and didn't eat fresh "eggs" every morning? What if Alanna and I didn't have artwork of me being a "hand trained for war"? What if I walked outside and didn't hear the "pop pop pop" of nail guns? What if I hadn't "sat in the freedom of Jesus" in "the very nice woods" in the middle of "the night"? The messages would not have made sense.

How about my "naps"? Or my writing a chapter titled "First Fruits"? Or praying in the house at night while it was under construction, popping to Papa? That was a huge one!

What about "old Perry"? And my cry to God that things were "blurry"?

Or my discussion with Chris, or my index card from Alanna, both saying I should "stay in my lane," only to have it confirmed word for word by Josiah's message right afterward?

There was more, so much more, and every time I went back through the printed pages, I found tidbits that seemed less important earlier but now jumped out at me. Each detail was highly unique. A physics teacher told me the mathematical odds of all these details randomly fitting one person were practically impossible.

There was the possibility, of course, that I was delusional. Those who thought I made the whole thing up were entitled to believe that, but they were wrong. I had witnesses. Plus, I couldn't make up a story like this if I tried. Granted, it was a mystery that was hard to wrap my mind around, but there was one thing that was hard to argue with—those pesky little facts!

I simply couldn't reason it away. With a keen drive for truth, my intellect and integrity forced me to come to the same conclusion as before. This entire encounter with Josiah was a God thing. I had no other explanation.

I also came to a conclusion as to why God allowed suffering.

I…didn't…know.

God was God. I was not.

Of course, the biblical explanation is that we live in a fallen world where bad things happen, and God is in the process of restoring it. When Jesus comes again, He will set up His kingdom. For now, He redeems our circumstances and comforts us as we go through painful situations. This world is not our ultimate home. God is real, is alive, is fully present, and works through broken people such as me and Josiah.

It is only human to wrestle with these questions. In God's Word, He never denies this world is broken. Over and over again, He tells it just like it is. Evil entered the world, the curse happened, and both seem to have the upper hand for a period of time. Bad things happen to people who try to do right. Life is not fair. Pain and suffering exist. At times it seems God is sitting on the sidelines, twiddling His thumbs, or doesn't exist at all.

Nothing reflects this like the story of John the Baptist. While John was still in his mother's womb, the Holy Spirit came upon him, and he leapt as Mary, pregnant with Jesus, walked into the room. Once grown, John preached repentance and baptism, leading the way for Jesus the Messiah. He baptized Jesus and witnessed the Holy Spirit descending on Him like a dove. "He must increase, but I must decrease," John said after that.[1] "Assuredly, I say to you," Jesus said, "among those born of women there has not risen one greater than John the Baptist."[2] John was clearly anointed and appointed by God, with the Holy Spirit upon him.

Fast-forward a bit, and John is sitting in a cold, dark dungeon awaiting his execution. Death by beheading was certainly not what he had expected with the Messiah now on the earth. Wasn't Jesus supposed to set up His earthly kingdom? John began having serious doubts and sent two messengers to ask Jesus, "Are You the Coming One, or do we look for another?"[3]

Really, John? After all you had witnessed, you just had to ask?

Yes, even this man of God, none greater by Jesus' own words, found himself in prison and questioning if Jesus was really who He said He was. The dark dungeons of life have a way of doing that to us. So does sickness, unemployment, death of a loved one, autism, and countless other things. Suffering blurs the truth at times.

But watch Jesus' response after John's messengers caught up with Him. "Go and tell John the things which you hear and see: The blind see and the lame walk; the lepers are cleansed and the deaf hear; the dead are raised up and the poor have the gospel preached to them. And blessed is he who is not offended because of Me."[4]

What? Are you kidding? That was all Jesus had to say to His devoted servant in the depths of his most intense suffering?

Apparently it was. And Jesus didn't rescue John either!

In fact, He left him in prison and let things play out. It didn't make sense. Jesus healed blind eyes, walked on water, multiplied the loaves and fishes, and raised the dead. Certainly He could have delivered His own cousin to spare his life. At first glance, it seemed Jesus was uncaring, unkind, and detached and didn't feel John's pain. Yet that couldn't be true. Jesus loved John the Baptist.

No; there was something bigger going on. An epic battle was raging in the spirit world. Things that were blurred in the present would become clear later on. John had to believe by faith in the Word of God just as all of us do. Actually, the first part of Jesus' response to John was scripture from Isaiah 61, prophesying of

Himself. And did you catch that last line of Jesus' response, "Blessed is he who is not offended because of Me"?

Jesus was telling John, "Hold fast to what you have witnessed and experienced. Refresh your mind with My words. Realign your thoughts with what you know is true about Me." He was letting John know something bigger was going on. Even though it didn't make sense and seemed as if he were being abandoned, he wasn't. "Don't let the fact that I'm not rescuing you offend you, John. Don't get mad at Me. Trust Me. Trust the Word of God." God is telling us the same thing today.[5]

The apostle Paul reminds us that in the present world we see through a glass dimly. Things just might get blurry. We know in part now, but one day we'll have full knowledge.[6]

I don't know why Josiah still suffers from autism. I wish he didn't.

Yet my encounter with him clearly displayed the reality of the other dimension. God sees and He cares. Just because it seems He is silent doesn't mean He is not listening.

Like John the Baptist, maybe you're still waiting to experience a supernatural deliverance, encounter, or miracle, but this doesn't mean your faith is weak or God isn't fully present. He is. This life is really about eternity. God is *real*, and there *is* an actual heaven. If you know Jesus, your end will truly be blessed. And God sees that from an eternal perspective even the worst day of your life can actually be your best day.

March 2019

In early spring I self-published this story as a little book. I normally don't self-publish, but in this case I and others I trusted felt specifically led that I should just get the message out and believe the Holy Spirit would take it to the next level.

The response was crazy! After reading the story, people wept.

Many wrote us, telling how their lives were deeply impacted. Alanna and I knew God was doing something special.

I realized there also were some potentially dangerous things about a book like this, and I tried to be wise in my approach. Some readers could wonder, "Why don't experiences like your story happen to me?" Others might think, "I must be *less than* and have weak faith because I haven't gotten any messages or had visions."

The truth is, we all move into God's presence by faith in His promises, not by feelings or experiences. Surely all of us go through seasons of dryness. Jesus said, "Blessed are those who have not seen and yet have believed."[7] Pastor Robert Morris of Gateway Church wrote:

> Sometimes a person in a deep relationship with God will be trusted with a time of God's silence. This person may be walking closely and carefully with the Lord, but will experience no communication that can be recognized as from God, other than the Bible itself.[8]

So perhaps those who persist, even though they don't experience some supernatural encounter, are actually more faithful and have a higher level of trust placed on them.

All I know is I will be held responsible for the gift God gave me. "To whom much is given," the scripture says, "from him much will be required."[9] I take this responsibility very soberly. Maybe I was graced with this Josiah encounter because of my own issues. Who knows! I am definitely flawed and very human.

Out of obedience, I began compiling my Josiah stories into book form. I knew it was my assignment from the Lord, whether or not publishers or industry people got the point. It wasn't about me but about Jesus being alive and using a willing, open, unfiltered vessel like Josiah.

The fact remains that the encounter did happen. I wrote and published it to encourage others on their own spiritual journeys.

Regardless of what you are going through, even when you don't understand, God is real, alive, and fully present. He has every hair on your head numbered, exactly as the Bible says, and He hears you the moment you start "Papaing."

October 2019

The little book was selling quickly, changing hearts and lives, and I saw no need to get in the way of what God was doing. Then I had an unexpected and divine appointment to meet with Charisma House. The publisher had read the story and loved it. Charisma acquired the book, planning to take it to the next level, just as Alanna and I believed the Holy Spirit promised would happen. I was asked to do a rewrite, with the new edition set for release in 2021.

"What?" I thought. That was a long time to wait. Why not in early 2020?

"Be patient," I heard the Holy Spirit whisper. "It is for My perfect time."

At that point I was planning to teach at a prayer conference in Minneapolis in January and was hoping to see Josiah and his parents one more time. None of us had yet heard of COVID-19.

The Bible's brutal honesty about suffering in this world is one of the reasons I personally believe. The same is true for many former agnostics and atheists, such as C. S. Lewis, who wrote:

> Reality, in fact, is usually something you could not have guessed. That is one of the reasons I believe Christianity. It is a religion you could not have guessed. If it offered us just the kind of universe we had always expected, I should feel we were making it up. But, in fact, it is not the sort of thing anyone would have made up....What is the problem? A universe that contains much that is obviously bad and apparently

meaningless, but containing creatures like ourselves who know that it is bad and meaningless....[It's] a good world that has gone wrong, but still retains the memory of what it ought to have been.[10]

God didn't just point out the dilemma of our species, but He did something radical. He became one of us and entered into our human sufferings! Jesus knows what it is to feel pain, real pain, both physical and emotional. The Father knows what it is like to see His child suffer. God entered this world as a human to redeem humanity, right a universe gone wrong, and purge evil from His creation.

One day every sickness and disease will be healed.

All tears will be wiped away.

Evil and sin will no longer exist.

In the meantime, miracles sometimes still happen. Over my years as a journalist, I've seen too much to deny it. Faith and trust are important elements, because in our brokenness and frailty God still shows up, bringing us hope, peace, and comfort. It is because of brokenness and frailty that this story of a non-verbal autistic boy and a quirky ole writer even happened.

It's the story of three: Jesus, Josiah, and me.

19

HE *IS* THE REWARD

*It was as if a great Presence walked into my room in
those early morning hours and sat down near me....
And this God—your Friend—wants to abide with you
even more than you want to abide with Him.*

—BRUCE WILKINSON, *SECRETS OF THE VINE*

January 11, 2020

MY INCREDIBLE JOURNEY with Josiah had started five
years earlier—five years and three days, to be exact. That
weekend I was back in Minneapolis, speaking on prayer at a
church, and Tahni Cullen was in attendance. As soon as I was
done, I'd pay Josiah my second visit.

Once again, Joe and Tahni welcomed me into their home. We
had a nice conversation, and my expectations were much more
realistic this time around.

"Josiah's body," Tahni updated me, "is in absolute overdrive.
He is making this horrible sound, along with clapping, stomping,
constant noise, and not able to hardly wind down until very late
at night and early morning. We can barely go anywhere anymore
with him until he gets this horrible scream under control."

Josiah was amazing *and* his condition was crushing, all at the
same time. God's grace is sufficient, but the trials people face are
difficult and painful.

When I went into Josiah's room to see him, my heart broke.
He had grown another foot and was clearly going through the
physical changes of puberty. Regarding the autism, he was in
another phase and more locked up. His parents told me he was
still unable to go online by himself and couldn't even turn the

pages of a book. I could see how badly he wanted to communicate with me. His struggle to type was intense this time, much more than before.

Tahni held up the laminated keyboard. "Do you want to say something to Max?"

Josiah indicated he wanted to proceed. He touched his finger to a letter and stopped.

"Jo," Tahni said, "do you want to keep going?"

He moaned, pointed to a letter or two or three, then stopped again.

Tahni asked quietly if he wanted to go on.

This continued for what seemed like an eternity. Watching from the beanbag, I could see every letter typed and every ounce of effort involved. Even as an observer, I found the process tedious, and it was obvious Tahni was physically drained and emotionally worn. This was not fun. It was a battle.

In addition to caring for Josiah 24/7, Tahni was caretaking her mother, who was now living with them and battling cancer. I was so grateful to this family for allowing me into their world. My pages of messages from Josiah were a treasure, a labor of pure love and obedience to the Holy Spirit. Emotion caught in my throat, and I fought back tears.

Finally, after all the struggle, he typed a couple of sentences:

> Old Perry, typing you a note reflects our eager affect. Eager understanding nominates you. You totally helped hand family understanding in my poetic offerings. Yes, our eager likes definitely only answer to God. Am I more yes than no meeting sorry Mom.

I had to smile at Josiah's use of "Old Perry." Already, God had done a lot of healing in that area of my past. Josiah also wanted me to know that my validation of his words had helped his family's "understanding" of his "poetic offerings." In the last part

Josiah assured his mom he liked this "meeting" with me and he was "sorry" it was so taxing on her.

Again, it was heartwarming and heartbreaking all at the same time.

———

Summer 2020

The deadline for this book was four days away. The year's events were so chaotic and painful, one of the most devastating in our history, and we had just come out of three months of COVID-19 quarantine. People needed the message of this book more than ever.

Then the riots and destruction hit. Cities were in flames, the economy was at a standstill, and the country was in turmoil like I'd never seen in my lifetime. The news that particular day was exceptionally horrible. I couldn't believe what was unfolding before my eyes. Another wave of the virus was projected, extending the lockdown, and the violence in the streets hyper-escalated.

I just wept, thinking of my grandkids and the world they were growing up in. "He reads tearful magazines of news" kept coming to my mind. How accurately Josiah had described me.

"Stop watching the news," Alanna told me. "It's derailing you."

She was right. God was blessing us, and I had plenty of work to do. I climbed into my truck and left to run some errands. When I got home, I planned to spend the rest of the day outside writing in the beautiful weather.

Still, I was fighting depression. Only one thing could keep me from losing my sanity. It was getting into God's presence. I had to stop whatever I was doing and dive into one of my secret places with Him. That was what David did. "O God, You are my God; early will I seek You; My soul thirsts for You; My flesh longs for You in a dry and thirsty land where there is no water.

So I have looked for You in the sanctuary, to see Your power and Your glory."[1] David understood there was power and glory in the presence of the Lord. God's power empowers us.

This all sounded good as I drove, but because of all the unrest, I felt myself shutting down, paralyzed by the pain in our country. I knew the source of my security, and I wasn't lacking faith or walking in fear, yet I was hurting.

It is indeed possible to experience faith and pain at the same time. When Jesus saw Mary mourning over her brother Lazarus' death, He felt deep grief and He wept. He wept for her pain and His own, even though Lazarus was about to be raised from the dead.[2]

All I could think about was getting back to my war room, and I whipped my truck around. Once inside my office, I jerked the curtains shut, grabbed my guitar, and just cried out to God in worship, unleashing all my deep feelings. I didn't just cry; I wailed. Tears are a language God understands. He knows our circumstances. Sometimes tears are the Holy Spirit praying through us, and when that happens, it is best to just *lean into it*. No words are needed.

While worshipping, I heard the Holy Spirit tell me, "Pick up your pen and write."

Boom! Like a gift, words for this chapter came flooding in. I wasn't looking for them, but as a result of my crying out for more of Jesus, He was speaking something to me.

And what was that message?

Regardless of our circumstances or how we feel, God sees us. He knows where we are and what we are going through. He is still speaking to His people, and ultimate peace and power come from His presence. We need that presence more than ever to carry us through this day and time. Just like Moses only moved forward if God's presence was with him, we too have to march into this unknown and volatile future with His presence.[3] It's the only way.

During the year I was given to rewrite this book, I kept asking God for another prophetic message from Josiah—just one more, please, just one more. It would wrap this book up with a nice little bow.

But nothing—not a peep, nada, zip. Silence.

Despite two great visits to the Cullens in Minnesota and the sense they were now family, I received no more personal prophetic words from Josiah. Just as God had spoken to me through the boy's messages, He now spoke to me through the boy's silence.

The Holy Spirit was telling me to move on from Josiah. That season had helped me through a difficult time, and I had been gifted with a message of hope for others. But now it was over. The Cullens would always be a big part of my life, and if God decided to speak to me again through Josiah, great, but I couldn't seek that from him. God wasn't warning me against expecting the miraculous but against the temptation to *worship* the miraculous.

The Israelites made this mistake after God gave them a physical item as a symbol of His healing. Poisonous snakes were attacking them in the wilderness, and many died. They pleaded with Moses to save them, and God instructed Moses to make a bronze serpent and put it on a pole. Anyone who looked to it in faith would be healed[4]—not by works but by grace alone. It was a foreshadowing of Jesus, who was lifted up on the cross. "And as Moses lifted up the serpent in the wilderness, even so must the Son of Man be lifted up, that whoever believes in Him should not perish but have eternal life."[5]

The interesting thing was the Israelites eventually turned the bronze serpent into an idol, burning incense to it and worshipping it instead of God. Years later the very thing used as an instrument to bring forth a miracle had to be destroyed.[6] God doesn't want us making idols out of experiences, prophetic words, or people He uses—even a young autistic boy.

The apostle Paul had many supernatural encounters. Jesus

appeared to him on the road to Damascus. He had an out-of-body trip to heaven. Angels appeared to him. He had visions and dreams. Prison doors flung open when he sang praises. And he saw many miracles wrought through his hands. Paul certainly shared these stories to encourage people, but the encounters were not his goals. Paul's goal was to *know* Jesus intimately. In Philippians 3:10 he said, "that I may know him and the power of his resurrection." The word *know* in the Greek means to know in a personal relationship.

Do you realize God wants to *know you*?

You've come a long way with me, and this book is almost over, but God's work is just beginning. He wants to open your eyes, mind, and heart to Him in deeper, unimaginable ways. He wants you to sit in the freedom of Jesus, beholding His face. He wants you to crawl up into Papa's lap with His Book. While you sit in His lap, the Holy Spirit wants to breathe life into the words of His Book, revealing His truths for you. This is where you belong.

Often we want tasks and purpose. We want ministries and assignments.

First, we must want Him.

Our primary ministry is to love Him above all else.

However we do it, getting into the secret place of God's presence is the most important thing we will ever do. Knowing Him *is* our purpose. Assignments are what He gives us. Out of His presence come peace, joy, love, wisdom, direction, and assignments.

Here's the crazy, wonderful thing: experiencing more *of* Him in relationship naturally leads to more *from* Him that empowers our lives. David Brainerd, a missionary to Native Americans in the 1700s, wrote, "Spent much time in prayer in the woods and seemed raised above the things of this world."[7]

That afternoon, back in my office, it was God's presence that raised me above the concerns of viruses, lockdowns, and riots and gave me courage to take another step forward—not just to survive but to thrive.

"But those who wait on the Lord," wrote Isaiah, "shall renew their strength; they shall mount up with wings like eagles, they shall run and not be weary, they shall walk and not faint."[8] Waiting on God is not a passive thing. The Hebrew word in Isaiah translated "wait" is *qavah*. It means "to wait, look for, hope, expect...bind together."[9] Think about it—waiting on Him is about binding together with Him. Those who "bind together" with Him shall renew their strength!

Looking back, I realized Josiah's messages never brought attention to him and always pointed me toward connecting with Jesus. My relationship with God was the central thread that tied all his words together:

> My Jesus wants note takers to name him as a king....
> Jesus is best known through his nails....My brag-
> ging is this. Jesus is big to my name but I am small
> to deserve his wonderful saving....He is so loudly
> in love with you....He must be going to your night
> prayer, you made an altar for him there....This call
> today is creating freedom in you. Jesus felt a very big
> hello....Hearing big papaing is very nightly fantastic
> to papa....Papa is looking at you too....God brightens
> his home in Heaven with your joy.

All along, Jesus was wooing me to pursue and find Him. As much as I desired an encounter with Him, Jesus desired an encounter with *me*.

"If we draw near to God," James wrote, "He will draw near to us."[10]

What does that mean, though? According to Scripture, He is already near. How can we draw near if He is already living inside us? "In Him we live and move and have our being," Paul told us. In the preceding verse, he said, "so that they should seek the Lord, in the hope that they might grope for Him and find Him, though He is not far from each one of us."[11] God is near to all of us, and

He wants us to seek after Him, to grope for Him. Groping is an indication of desperation. When we do, He shows up.

A. W. Tozer explained it perfectly:

> The Presence and the manifestation of the Presence are not the same. There can be the one without the other. God is here when we are wholly unaware of it. He is *manifest* only when and as we are aware of His Presence. On our part there must be surrender to the Spirit of God, for His work it is to show us the Father and the Son. If we co-operate with Him in loving obedience God will manifest Himself to us, and that manifestation will be the difference between a nominal Christian life and a life radiant with the light of His face.[12]

God *wants* to reveal more of Himself to us. Our job is to block out the distractions and pulls from this world so we can listen for His still, small promptings. Like a divine dance, our lives shift from performance-based religion and activities to having our eyes locked on Jesus in love, our arms firmly embracing Him in order to follow His lead, stepping where He steps, stopping where He stops, fully trusting when He twirls and dips us.

Jesus is real, alive, and fully present. He wants us to seek more *of* Him, not more *from* Him. "He is a rewarder of those who diligently seek Him," says the writer of Hebrews.[13]

He hears and sees us. He longs for an intimate relationship with us.

From that intimacy with Him, from His presence, flows everything else we need.

Make an altar for Him.

He *is* the reward.

God is a good gift giver.
—Josiah Cullen

Appendix

BEGIN A RELATIONSHIP WITH
JESUS CHRIST TODAY

THE FIRST STEP in God's will for your life is for you to be reconciled to Him. That means to be connected in fellowship with the One who created you. Jesus' sacrifice on the cross made a way for this to happen. Before you can be restored, however, you must understand you are separated from God because of your sin.

What is sin? It is doing anything that is wrong according to God's standard, or not doing what is right by that same standard. First John 1:8 says, "If we say that we have no sin, we deceive ourselves, and the truth is not in us." Romans 3:23 states, "For all have sinned and fall short of the glory of God." The good news is, regardless of your past, Jesus' blood can cleanse you and set your life on a new course. John 3:16 says, "For God so loved the world that He gave His only begotten Son, that whoever believes in Him should not perish but have everlasting life."

God does not want any of us to perish and live in eternal darkness and separation from Him. He wants to give us new and everlasting life. That life begins when we put our faith in what Jesus did for us on the cross. Faith is not simply mental acknowledgment but trusting totally in the hope of what Jesus accomplished for us and embracing His promises. When we do this, God forgives our sins, cleanses us, and puts His Spirit within us.

Jesus said in John 3:3, "Most assuredly, I say to you, unless one is born again, he cannot see the kingdom of God." If God's Spirit, the Holy Spirit of Jesus, is not inside you, then you are in essence a walking dead man. Yes, you are alive physically, but your spirit man is dead. When Adam sinned, he immediately died spiritually and then eventually died physically. Being born again is what happens when we receive God's gift of eternal, everlasting life and His Spirit comes to dwell in us. Our spirit man comes to life. This is a gift we receive by faith.

"For the wages of sin is death," says Romans 6:23, "but the gift of God is eternal life in Christ Jesus our Lord." Romans 5:17 adds, "Those who receive abundance of grace and of the gift of righteousness will reign in life through the One, Jesus Christ." John 1:12 states, "But as many as received Him, to them He gave the right to become children of God, to those who believe in His name." Romans 10:9–10 says, "If you confess with your mouth the Lord Jesus and believe in your heart that God has raised Him from the dead, you will be saved. For with the heart one believes unto righteousness, and with the mouth confession is made unto salvation."

PRAYER TO RECEIVE JESUS AND BE BORN AGAIN

Jesus, I recognize I am a sinner, separated from You. I believe You are the Son of God. I believe You died on the cross for my sins and rose again to restore me to a relationship with You. Right now I receive Your gift of forgiveness and new life. Wash me and cleanse me. Come into my heart. Fill me with Your love, Your peace, and Your life. Live in me and love through me for the rest of my life. Thank You, God. In Jesus' name I pray. Amen.

If you prayed this with sincere faith, then God's Spirit came inside you. Ephesians 1:13 says, "In Him you also trusted, after you heard the word of truth, the gospel of your salvation; in whom also, having believed, you were sealed with the Holy Spirit of promise." It is a promise to be believed regardless of how you feel. Your next step is to grow daily in your faith by reading the Bible, praying, and being in fellowship with other believers. The Holy Spirit will transform you from the inside out. It's a process. It's not always spectacular, but it is supernatural!

ACKNOWLEDGMENTS

A PROJECT SUCH AS this would never be birthed without the help of many selfless and gifted people. I express my sincere gratitude to:

Marcos Perez, for catching the vision for this book and your ongoing support. You are the fulfillment of the Holy Spirit's word, "Watch what I do. Then you will have your answer."

Kyle Duncan, for doing what you do and being my friend. You're a mover and a shaker, and your energy is contagious!

Adrienne Gaines, for your editorial wisdom, patience, and kind heart.

Eric Wilson. What a gifted writer and editor you are! Thank you for helping me take the manuscript to the stratosphere. I loved working with you. You have made me better.

Charisma, the entire team.

Bruce Van Natta. God has used you so many times in my life that I'm losing count. We need another visit.

Germaine Copeland. What a joy to get to know you. You have impacted millions of lives for prayer and have impacted mine. I'm humbled and honored that you read and endorsed this book.

Kyle Loffelmacher. You rock! You have no idea how much your encouragement, advice, and friendship have meant to me. You are special.

All the readers of the original version who bought copies, shared them with others, and let me know how the story deeply impacted you. Your endorsements and testimonies inspired me to keep going. There are too many of you to name individually, but know that you were gasoline to my fire. Thank you!

Michelle Jester, my heroine for the layout, website, social media, marketing, and other online issues, for always making time for me, especially at short notice.

Joe and Tahni Cullen, for sharing your son with me and allowing me to enter your lives. You guys will always be family to me.

Josiah. Thank you for hearing God's voice and sharing your messages with me. We are banded together for life.

Cheryl Ricker. You are a great writer in your own right. I'll always be grateful for you connecting me to Josiah.

Alanna, my wife, best friend, and wielder. Simply put, your name should be on all my books. I love you!

ABOUT THE AUTHOR

Max Davis is the author of over thirty books. In addition to his own works, he has done numerous collaborations with highly notable leaders. Max's books have been featured in *USA Today*, *Publishers Weekly*, and *Southern Living* and on Bible Gateway, *The Today Show*, and *The 700 Club*. He holds degrees in journalism and biblical studies and is a faith-energizing speaker for churches and organizations. God is using Max's hope-infused stories combined with journalistic research and solid biblical teaching to challenge unbelievers, encourage those struggling in their faith, and spark prayer revivals in hearts around the world. He lives in south Louisiana under an umbrella of oaks with his wife and best friend, Alanna.

For weekly encouragement, including videos, follow Max on Facebook and Twitter. Also, for other books and speaking information, check out MaxDavisBooks.com.

facebook.com/maxdavisauthor

@maxdavisbooks

NOTES

PREFACE

1. Henry and Richard Blackaby and Claude King, *Experiencing God* (Nashville: Broadman & Holman Publishers, 2008).

CHAPTER 4

1. 2 Kings 3:15–16, ESV.
2. 2 Chronicles 20:21–22, NIV.
3. Acts 16:25–26.
4. Matthew 6:6, NIV.
5. Psalm 77:11, MSG.

CHAPTER 5

1. See 1 Corinthians 12:12–19.
2. Ephesians 2:10.

CHAPTER 6

1. Matthew 11:30.
2. James 4:2.
3. James 4:3.
4. 2 Corinthians 13:5.

CHAPTER 7

1. "Lining Mine Shafts," *Scientific American*, October 23, 1915, https://www.scientificamerican.com/article/lining-mine-shafts/.
2. "Shaft Mining," Wikipedia, September 8, 2020, https://en.wikipedia.org/wiki/Shaft_mining#Shaft_lining.
3. M. Jendryś, "Analysis of Stress State in Mine Shaft Lining, Taking Into Account Superficial Defects," IOP Publishing, accessed September 8, 2020, https://iopscience.iop.org/article/10.1088/1755-1315/261/1/012016/pdf.
4. See Matthew 26:69–75.
5. John 21:16–17, NIV.
6. Romans 5:17, NIV.
7. John 3:18.
8. Zephaniah 3:17, ESV.

CHAPTER 8

1. Philippians 4:7.
2. Charles Spurgeon, "921. Nathanael and the Fig Tree" (a sermon delivered March 20, 1870, at Metropolitan Tabernacle, Newington, UK), Answers in Genesis, December 16, 2011, https://answersingenesis.org/education/spurgeon-sermons/921-nathanael-and-the-fig-tree/.

CHAPTER 9

1. James 4:6.

CHAPTER 10

1. See 1 Corinthians 14:14–15 for more on speaking in tongues.
2. Dictionary.com, s.v. "bite," accessed November 11, 2020, https://www.dictionary.com/browse/bite.
3. *Merriam-Webster*, s.v. "sink one's teeth into," accessed November 11, 2020, https://www.merriam-webster.com/thesaurus/sink%20one%27s%20teeth%20into.
4. Hebrews 4:16; 10:19–22.

CHAPTER 11

1. Psalm 42:1, NIV.
2. John 4:14, NIV.
3. C. S. Lewis, *Mere Christianity* (New York: Simon & Schuster/Touchstone, 1980).
4. John Piper, *Desiring God, Revised Edition* (Colorado Springs, CO: Multnomah Books, 2011), 100.
5. Nehemiah 8:10.
6. See Nehemiah 4:14.
7. Anne McCain and Amy L. Sherman, *Effective Advocacy: Ten Principles From Nehemiah* (n.p.), https://fhadvocates.files.wordpress.com/2009/06/nehemiah-booklet1.pdf.
8. John 15:11.
9. Andrew Murray, *Abide in Christ* (London: James Nisbet & Co., 1888), 176.
10. Exodus 33:14–15.

CHAPTER 12

1. Bill Kynes, PhD, "Growing in Prayer Part 1: Hindrances to Prayer," C. S. Lewis Institute, November 20, 2016,

https://www.cslewisinstitute.org/Growing_in_Prayer_
Part_1_Hindrances_to_Prayer_page1.

2. Scott G. Wilkins, "The Role of the Pastor in Evangelism,"
   Christianity Today, September 9, 2020, https://www.
   christianitytoday.com/pastors/2007/july-online-
   only/031306.html.

3. "Create Your Own Spiritual Hot Spot," Karen Hardin,
   accessed September 3, 2020, http://www.karenhardin.
   com/create-your-own-spiritual-hot-spot/.

4. Psalm 16:8, NIV.

5. "Why Are Grapes Harvested at Night?," Mirabeau,
   March 1, 2015, https://www.mirabeauwine.com/about-
   wine/grapes-harvested-night/.

6. Lisa Mattson, "Five Reasons Why Wineries Night
   Harvest Chardonnay Grapes," Jordan Winery, accessed
   September 3, 2020, https://winecountrytable.com/eat-
   drink/wine-101/five-reasons-wineries-night-harvest-
   grapes.

7. Fergal Gleeson, "The Night Shift: Ensuring a Good
   Vintage by Picking at Night," Your Margaret River
   Region, March 29, 2018, https://www.margaretriver.com/
   stories-the-night-shift/.

CHAPTER 13

1. Lexico, s.v. "hosanna," accessed November 10, 2020,
   https://www.lexico.com/en/definition/hosanna.

CHAPTER 14

1. Roy Hicks Jr., *Small Book About God* (Sisters, OR:
   Multnomah, 1997), 60.

2. Genesis 41:26–27.

3. See Hebrews 4:15.

4. See Psalm 103:14.

5. See Matthew 18:12.

CHAPTER 15

1. Acts 16:9–10, NIV.

CHAPTER 16

1. 1 Corinthians 9:24.

2. Hebrews 12:1–2, NLT.

CHAPTER 17

1. 2 Peter 1:16.

CHAPTER 18

1. John 3:30.
2. Matthew 11:11.
3. Matthew 11:3.
4. Matthew 11:4–6.
5. Max Davis, *When Jesus Was a Green-Eyed Brunette: Loving People Like God Does* (Nashville: Worthy Publishers, 2016).
6. 1 Corinthians 13:12.
7. John 20:29.
8. Robert Morris, *Frequency* (Nashville: Thomas Nelson, 2016), 142.
9. Luke 12:48.
10. Lewis, *Mere Christianity*, 48.

CHAPTER 19

1. Psalm 63:1–2.
2. See John 11:23–35.
3. See Exodus 33:14–15.
4. See Numbers 21:6–9.
5. John 3:14–15.
6. 2 Kings 18:3–4.
7. Fred Barlow, *Profiles in Evangelism* (Murfreesboro, TN: Sword of the Lord Publishers, 1976), 34.
8. Isaiah 40:31.
9. Blue Letter Bible, s.v. "*qavah*," accessed September 3, 2020, https://www.blueletterbible.org/lang/Lexicon/Lexicon.cfm?strongs=H6960&t=KJV.
10. James 4:8.
11. Acts 17:27–28.
12. A. W. Tozer, *The Pursuit of God* (Harrisburg, PA: Christian Publications, 1948), https://www.gutenberg.org/files/25141/25141-h/25141-h.htm.
13. Hebrews 11:6.